ALL WHO LIVE ON ISLA[

# ALL WHO

# LIVE ON

# ISLANDS

陆杨怡 | Rose Lu

Victoria University Press

Victoria University of Wellington Press
PO Box 600 Wellington
New Zealand
vup.wgtn.ac.nz

A catalogue record is available from the
National Library of New Zealand.

ISBN 9781776562893

Printed by Markono Print Media, Singapore

*for Matthew*

# CONTENTS

# 穷人店、富人店

*Beep!* The buzzer in the dairy goes off. I leave the lounge, walk through the kitchen and trot down the corridor, arriving at the internal door that separates our house from the dairy. On this journey I change my 拖鞋 | slippers twice, from the lounge pair to the house pair, then from the house pair to the shop pair.

My mum is sitting on one of the two stools behind the counter. The seat is upholstered with tan faux leather, cracked and patchy. She hands me the car keys.

"小怡, 带爷爷奶奶去买点儿水果。" | "Rose, can you take your grandparents shopping for fruit?"

"好吧, 去哪儿个店?" | "Sure, which shop?"

"穷人店吧。" | "Let's do the poor-person shop, eh?"

"Okay."

I climb back up the concrete steps and head back to the lounge, observing the slipper ritual in reverse. As usual, my grandparents are sitting in the La-Z-Boys. I've never known what colour they are, as they've had heavy curtain fabric draped over them since they were purchased. Kon-kon's eyes

9

are shut and my brother's baby blanket is covering his knees. Bu'uah is sitting with her hands clasped, leaning forward with her milky eyes fixed to the television.

"Bu'uah, 'ng da ni ken Kon-kon ki 'ma sy-ku." | "Bu'uah, I'll take you and Kon-kon to buy fruit," I say.

With my grandparents, I speak tshon-min 'eu | Chóngmíng dialect. There are three languages in this house, and each generation favours a different one.

Bu'uah stands up, pressing down the creases on the front of her shirt. "Au, 'ng-li ki jion-nyng-die 'ai-dzi fu-nyng-die?" | "Okay, are we going to the poor-person shop or the rich-person shop?"

"Jion-nyng-die." | "The poor-person shop."

Her half-moon eyes crinkle as she smiles at me. She grabs the remote and silences her period drama.

No motion from Kon-kon. Maybe he hasn't heard? I give him the benefit of the doubt. His sudden onset of deafness had caught me by surprise, cautioning that I should come home more frequently. Bu'uah takes a few steps towards him. The foam bottoms of her 拖鞋 | slippers make a scraping sound on the carpet.

"Ki 'ma sy-ku lie!" | "We're going to the shop!" she says. It's not quite a shout, but she speaks strongly.

His eyes open reluctantly. He shifts his farmer's hands from his knees to the armrest, leveraging all four limbs to come halfway out of the chair. A weak cough. Hands back on his knees to keep the fleece blanket from falling. A slow turn. He places the blanket on the back of the chair. Another cough. He tends to speak in dispassionate coughs these days.

I shuffle my grandparents out the door and into the eight-person people-mover that my parents own. It's silver and capacious. It even has a video feed showing the rear view while the car reverses. We got this car after we moved to Whanganui in 2003. Back in Auckland, if we ever went anywhere as a family, I had to sit on the floor between the back of the passenger's seat and the base of my baby brother's car seat. The adults were too big, my brother was too small, and we couldn't afford a new car. 没办法。

Whanganui's streets are luxuriously wide, even for this spaceship car. I would never be able to cruise like this down Wellington streets. Bu'uah sits up front with me, window cracked to stop her from getting motion sickness. My dad isn't allowed to drive if Bu'uah is in the car. His constant halting and lurching causes bile to crawl up her throat. It's just my mum and me whom she trusts. Kon-kon doesn't have the same issue, but he never wants to go anywhere.

We exit the roundabout onto London Street, then turn down Glasgow Street. I can see the building now—bright yellow and black over austere concrete. The poor-person shop looms over the other shops on the corner—Countdown, the Mad Butcher, Subway.

I park the car. We walk into the Pak'nSave.

The wildest deals of the day line the entranceway. Crown pumpkins with waxy blue-grey skin: two dollars. Not for a kilo but for the whole fat thing! Lindt chocolate bars, sea salt and caramel, short-dated and a measly buck each! Stacks of assorted Griffin's biscuits, practically given away at two for four dollars!

Bu'uah has already taken herself and a trolley through the clanging safety barrier that allows passage in one direction but not the other. Kon-kon takes his time entering, metal rods chiming individually as he ambles in.

A stand of white-fleshed peaches catches Bu'uah's eye. Their skins are a perfect blend of pink and white with a thin layer of mottled fuzz. She inspects the peaches, picking each one up and doing a full rotation to check for bruising. Satisfied, she places one in the plastic bag.

"Ge za dao-zi zai la le!" she exclaims, gesturing at the peaches, telling me that they're fantastic. She uses a word that doesn't have a Mandarin counterpart. I used to think that the dialect we spoke was only phonetically different, that I could map the eight tones into Mandarin's four, but I've realised that it has different vocabulary and grammar as well. They're not mutually intelligible.

"Ge za dao-zi ji kuan-nyeah?"| "How much are the peaches?" she asks. I know she can't read Mandarin, let alone English, but now I'm unsure if she can read numbers. Perhaps she can't match the numbers with the English signs? I tell her they are six dollars a kilo.

She nods, satisfied. The bag steadily fills as more peaches meet the requirements of her thorough inspection. She places the bag in the trolley and moves on to the next fruit.

After they have selected their desired fruit, I take them through the checkout. They wait patiently as each bag is weighed and placed into the new trolley.

"That comes to $23.56," says the checkout operator. I give her two twenty-dollar notes from my mum. She hands back the change and I put it straight into my pocket.

"Ge dei va?" | "Is the change correct?" Bu'uah points at my pocket with her crooked finger.

Once, I asked Bu'uah why her finger was like that. She told me that she was the youngest of the children in her family, and she loved eating sugarcane. One day she wanted to eat some, but none of her older siblings could be bothered hacking off a section for her. Exasperated, one of them told her to do it herself.

She took a cleaver to the woody cane, and accidentally cleaved off her fingertip. At this point in the retelling, she clutched her injured finger with the opposite hand and pretended to cry out for help. As if she were little again. As if the wound were still fresh.

Bu'uah looks at me.

"Dei ge!" | "Of course!" I reply, patting my cardigan pocket, not bothering to check.

Technically, my 爷爷奶奶 | grandparents are my 外公外婆 | grandparents—on my mother's side. I never liked how 外公 or 外婆 sounded. 外 translates to outside, foreign, external. As if they were standing outside our family, looking in but never participating. It didn't reflect how I felt about them, so I didn't address them that way.

They came to Aotearoa in late 1999, just after my brother was born. They would have been in their early sixties back then. My mum is an only child, so, unlike my dad's parents, her parents didn't need to split their attention between families.

I don't know many specifics about my grandparents, like exactly how old they are, or how to write their names. None of these details are important. Western birthday celebrations have never been a feature of our home life. They can speak their given names, but, like me, they don't know which characters make them up.

I call them Kon-kon (Grandpa) and Bu'uah (Grandma), and they call me Shiao-nyi-geu, a family nickname that means "little happy dog". I assume the middle character is taken from my Chinese name, but I don't know for sure. It's another name that is spoken rather than written.

Back in China they were farmers, the poorest class. It brings Bu'uah endless delight that the farmers here are affluent.

She can't understand how it's possible. Her sense of the vocation doesn't extend past the notion of planting crops as the single means to food, supplemented by a few chickens and maybe a goat in a good year.

In Whanganui Bu'uah is farming again, tending to her vegetable garden every day. They have a lot of time on their hands. Before we moved here, my brother hadn't started school, so my grandparents were kept busy caring for him while my parents worked.

My brother and I were born almost a decade apart and have grown up with completely different lives. Matthew goes to the private school in town, Whanganui Collegiate School. I went to the public school, Whanganui High School. Traditionally the 陆 | Lù family have been doctors, but my dad and his brother failed to get into med school and had to become engineers instead. Matthew is redeeming the Lù family line by pursuing health science at Otago University. I was accepted into the same course and hall of residence as him, but at the last minute I pulled out. I didn't know what I wanted to do but I knew it wasn't medicine.

Matthew is never asked to do chores for our grandparents. It's partly because he's too busy with school, but partly because he can't understand much tshon-min 'eu | Chóngmíng dialect. Mine isn't great either, but it's passable. Anything more complex than fruit prices requires me to switch to Mandarin. Thankfully, Bu'uah understands most of what I say. She spends a lot of time watching Chinese dramas with Mandarin dialogue, so she's picked a fair bit up.

Other than our excursions to the supermarket, the main activity I 陪 | accompany my grandparents in is playing cards. They have a set of long, thin Chinese cards. The backs are dark green, while the faces are adorned with black and white patterns according to their suit and value.

There are three suits in the deck—萬、条、筒 | wàn, tiáo and tóng, each running from one to nine. They symbolise different units of currency. Like old bank notes, the higher values are embossed with cursive red patterns. The three suits have shapes associated with them: small solid dots for 萬 | wàn, narrow segmented strips for 条 | tiáo, and patterned coins for 筒 | tóng.

The cards are designed to be stacked vertically, so players need only to glance at the top icons to read the value of the card. Groups of these card stacks are then nestled in the palm and held in place by a thumb across the short side. Because they're so long and thin, a certain deftness is needed just to hold them.

My grandparents play a variant of mahjong, which adapts its tile images from the faces in this deck. Most afternoons, I find them passing the time with this game. I sit down at the table with them.

Bu'uah looks up from her hand. "Be xiang va?" | "Do you want to play?"

"Au," I reply, and wait for them to finish the current round.

We've always been more of a cards family rather than a mahjong family. Back in 崇明 | Chóngmíng, Kon-kon played cards every day with his buddies. The air would be alive with curls of burnt tobacco, chain-smoked in an expression of manliness, and a spray of spittle and sunflower-seed shells fired from mouths. Now it's just Bu'uah he plays with, and me, when I'm home for the weekend.

It's hard to pinpoint when Kon-kon lost his voice. The Kon-kon that I remember from my childhood is a firecracker. We would play cards and he would always cheat, because he loved to win and he loved to make me laugh. The game was more about catching him at his cheating than about winning yourself.

He taught me nursery rhymes that only worked in 崇明 话 | Chóngmíng dialect, pinching the back of my hand with his hand, me pinching the back of his hand with my other hand, us repeating the pattern until all four of our hands were stacked and connected with plucked skin, at which point we would chant:

"Ma ha, ma ha!" | "Selling crabs, selling crabs!"

"Ma dao nin ga!" | "Selling crabs to other people!"

We could chant this two or three times before I collapsed into giggles, holding my hands up to look at the red markings stamped on the crab's shell.

This kon-kon was stubborn as well as vocal. He would complain about the food here because he thought the meat had a foreign smell. The staples he was used to were hard to come by. Even though what he'd eaten in China was poor farmer food, he preferred it. Western dishes were abhorrent. He had to be persuaded to try the prime steaks my parents bought. After just a few bites he announced that it was okay, but he preferred Chinese beef. This same New Zealand beef would be sold for upwards of 300元 a plate back in China.

He talked about how smart I was, how he still had the certificate of achievement I received in my first year of primary school. He was so proud of me. He unashamedly loved me the most, even though you're not supposed to pick a favourite grandchild, and, if you're Chinese, you're not supposed to pick the granddaughter.

Now he spends his days sitting in the La-Z-Boy, eyes shut with the blanket over his knees. He still opens his eyes when I come home, and for those moments his eyes light up. But on my last few trips I've noticed that after the initial greeting he shuts his eyes again and retreats back into himself. It's been a long time since he was energetic, but he used to at least ask how long I was home for, demand that I stay longer, and wheedle a date out of me for my next visit.

He doesn't get much respite from his daily routine of sitting and doing nothing. For him, there's not much worth engaging with. My parents are busy with the shop, my brother is busy with school, and my visits are limited. Stimulus disorients him, and he's always tired because he has insomnia. Playing cards is one of the only things he does during the day.

Kon-kon wins, so Bu'uah shuffles the cards. She cuts the bundle of cards into two neat piles, then threads one pile evenly through the other. I've tried this many times and have never got it right. The tips of the cards always clump together, resulting in an inadequate shuffle.

She lays the cards face down on the table, spreading them out slightly so they form a neat pleat. Like in mahjong, the cards are not dealt but picked up. Bu'uah is the leader this turn, and counts to herself as she picks them up.

"Yi ⋯⋯ nyi ⋯⋯ sae ⋯⋯ si ⋯⋯ 'n ⋯⋯ lo ⋯⋯ tchi ⋯⋯"

Sometimes she inserts a rhyme about the number, like a Daily Keno announcer—"Ba zha da yi da!"—before continuing on.

"Jyu ⋯⋯ sa ⋯⋯ sa-yi ⋯⋯ sa-nyi ⋯⋯ sa-sae ⋯⋯"

She announces the last number with a knock of her crooked finger on the table. "Sa-si!"

Kon-kon hasn't said a word. He no longer tries to hide cards up his sleeve. If he says anything, it's an admonishment for Bu'uah to hurry up. They bicker because they are an old married couple. Their days are spent with only each other, and outside of our family there is no one in Whanganui who can understand them.

I look at the cards in my hand. After a decade of playing,

I still can't determine their value solely by the iconography. Once the bundles are arranged neatly in my hand, I sometimes have to flick the cards forward to check their image for their worth. I have never seen my grandparents do this. They know this game inside out. Even as their other faculties dull, they remain skilled in strategy and card-counting.

Sometimes when we play, Bu'uah babbles about their old house and her old life back in China. She has no sense of time or sequence when she tells these stories. Her reminiscences about people and places can be nonsensical. Her thoughts are steeped in her superstitions and her lack of education, and she often comes to the wrong conclusions.

She left her entire family behind in Jiāngsū when she came to 崇明 | Chóngmíng to marry my kon-kon in her twenties; I know that for certain. I don't know any of her family members' names, but I've heard their oral obituaries.

She doesn't mean to be macabre in her recounting, the way she talks through precisely what her family members died of and how much they suffered; she simply tells the situation as she understands it. Medical jargon is a part of 崇明话 | Chóngmíng vocabulary that I am weak on, and other than cancer the causes of death are unknown to me. I don't know how she feels about these family members—she must not have seen them very often after she left. They all died at a much younger age than she is now.

Another of her favourite topics is her heavy winter coats. She remembers the 崇明 | Chóngmíng winter—the month or so when temperatures didn't rise above zero, the concrete housing, and the warm coats she wore. They had to leave the coats behind when they came to New Zealand. She pines for the coats, bought with money that was so hard-earned.

Bu'uah picks up a new card. She must like it, as she rearranges the stacks in her hand to tuck it away. With an exhalation, she discards a card, knocking her hand on the table again. My turn.

"Ae ⋯⋯ 'n di de van-zi la te le ⋯⋯" | "Ae, our house is rotting . . ." she laments.

I pick up a card and let her talk. As usual, her Chóngmíng dialect is croaky when discussing the past.

"We built the house with our own hands . . . we were so poor back in those days . . . your kon-kon used to cycle so far to work each day, getting up before the sun came up, and returning after the sun had set . . . we worked so hard and we were so hungry but there was no food so it was better to just go straight to sleep after work . . . those beautiful coats, also rotting in the house . . ."

Bu'uah's wishes are simple but also frustrating. She often has the same conversation with my mother, who gets more annoyed every time she has to explain the practicalities to her. "You can't just expect us to go and get your coats when we're in China! They're so bulky and heavy, we don't have the space to lug them around! And even if we did bring them back, then what? You can't even wear them here, it's too hot! We can buy you a coat here if you want!"

Bu'uah seems to have become more sentimental about the past in the last few years. Or maybe I've realised that there can't be that many more times I'll be able to hear these stories, this dialect. I think back to when I was younger, when Kon-kon was more vocal. Every time he complained about life in Aotearoa, Bu'uah would rise to its defence. "You imbecile! Look around you, look how clean it is! Everything is such good quality! This milk would cost a fortune in China!

What is there to miss, our grandchildren are here!"

I don't know if she feels so strongly now. Her grandchildren are grown and have vanished into a culture that she'll never be able to know, coming back with tone-deaf ears that don't understand her 土话 | unsophisticated dialect. Talking to her can feel crude and imprecise, like communicating through smoke signals.

Kon-kon picks up his card silently. He has nothing to contribute to Buʻuah's reminiscences, but maybe he can't hear what she's saying.

He discards; Buʻuah picks up. She discards.

I pick up. It's 三条 | three of tiáo, completing the last set in my hand, three-four-five of tiáo.

"Si mo!" | "I win!" I announce triumphantly.

Buʻuah cheers, clucking with laughter. "Ni xia-zha lai le, yi ze fe man ji te." | "You're so smart, you never forget how to play."

Buʻuah stops the game to prepare a salt wash for Kon-kon's foot. He has an ingrown toenail. It's the big toe on his left foot. It's made him even less active than he already is. The toe is a smash of yellow and pink, swollen with infection because he keeps picking at it. He's not supposed to. My mum took him to a podiatrist to get it cut, but the flesh was so puffy they couldn't do anything. The podiatrist told him to keep his hands away, soak the foot in hot brine to soften the nail, and they'll see if it's better at the next appointment.

But of course he refuses to stop picking, because he needs that temporary relief. He is a man who lives for instant gratification. He curses the doctors here. He complains to my mum. "What's the problem? The doctors here don't know how to do their job! Why can't they just anaesthetise my foot and cut the nail off? It's so simple!"

Kon-kon waits silently in his chair for the salt wash. He remains silent while Bu'uah brings in the orange plastic washtub, steaming hot. With a laboured sigh, he places his foot in the water. After scarcely ten minutes, he leans forward and reaches for the flannel.

"Ae!" Bu'uah makes a sound, but Kon-kon's foot is out now and he refuses to soak it any longer. "It's not going to do any good!" he barks at her, settling back in the chair and closing his eyes. No one can make him do anything he doesn't want to do.

My kon-kon is an insomniac. When I was a teenager I regularly stayed up until two or three in the morning, and on those nights I hoped he wouldn't notice the light emanating from under my door while he was on one of his night-time excursions. From my room I would hear the scuffle of his footsteps, his staccato cough. Next came the crinkle of soft packaging and the beep of the microwave. He'd say he couldn't sleep because he was hungry, but it's gone on for so long now that it's clearly become a bad habit.

Kon-kon is the only person in our family with a sweet tooth. His midnight snacks are sugary or fried, but preferably both. At his request my mum used to buy sweet fried dumplings on her monthly trips to the Chinese supermarket in Palmerston North. The dumplings were made from chewy glutinous rice flour, filled with creamy red bean paste or delicately salted pork mince, and deep-fried. By the time my mum was back in Whanganui, the oil from the dumplings would have soaked right through the brown paper bag.

Kon-kon is a diabetic. Glutinous rice is terrible for diabetics; its high glycaemic index causes sudden spikes in blood sugar, and the feeling of hunger comes back within an hour. After Kon-kon received his diagnosis, my mum stopped buying him the dumplings and other sugary snacks. So he started making his own snacks to eat during the night. Bloated 粽子 | sticky rice dumplings, bamboo wrappers barely containing the glutinous rice within. Flat, circular 汤圆 | tāngyuán, as big as my cupped palm, made from glutinous rice flour and filled with red bean paste. He'll wolf down at least three of these every night.

Kon-kon is eating himself to death and there is nothing we can do about it. Of course, this foot thing is related. His blood sugar levels in the morning hover around 15 mmol/L. A healthy reading is between 4mmol/L and 7mmol/L.

The first time my mum and Bu'uah saw that number, they were horrified. It was all because of his eating during the night, but he couldn't be persuaded to stop.

"I can't sleep if I'm hungry!" he would shout. "There is no worse feeling than lying in bed feeling hungry! Do you not want me to sleep?"

Scuff, scuff, scuff. My bu'uah pops her head into the lounge, staying in the kitchen so she doesn't have to swap out her 拖鞋 | slippers.

"Shiao-nyi-geu, bang 'n kai-ya-kai shi-yi-ji." | "Rose, help me turn on the washing machine."

My mum's mentioned before that my grandparents can't use the washing machine. I look at the panel. Coloured lights and options for wool and delicates. It can't be that hard, right? As long as they use the defaults.

I show her a few times. The small grey button to turn it on, the large green button to start and stop. She practises, nodding in acknowledgement.

The next time I come home, I see my mum helping Bu'uah with the washing machine again.

"Ng mang-ji te la?" | "Have you forgotten?"

"Pei! 'ng lao lai le yi yang a ji ve te!" | "Pei! I'm so old I can't remember anything!"

I used to think that my grandparents could spend a few years by themselves in China. When they were younger, they'd sometimes go back for years at a time. But I didn't realise how much that had changed as they got older.

My mum tells me about all the things they can't do. "我告诉你, 你的爷爷每天要打针。他的血糖量一直很高, 一起床已经超过十五了。奶奶也不能帮他打, 她没受过教育, 连洗衣机和吸尘器她也用不来。她每天看的电视也要我帮她打开。所以奶奶不能帮爷爷打针, 而且他们药也买不来。还有老家的邻居都搬走了或者去世了, 如果有问题也没有人可以帮他们。" | "Do you know that your kon-kon needs an insulin shot every day now? His blood sugar is so high, you know it's over fifteen when he wakes up. And do you think Bu'uah can give him his shots? Of course not. It's not her fault, she's never had any education. She can't even use the washing machine, or the vacuum cleaner. She can't use the TV she watches every day. I have to go in several times a day to change it to the right setting for her. There's no way she could give him his insulin shot. And where would they get the medication from? Who would they call if they needed help? All their neighbours are long dead, or gone to live with their families. There's no one to help them if they get in trouble."

She looks out at the dairy, at the fridges filled with candy drinks. It's the afternoon slump, the lull between the lunch rush and the after-school rush. My dad goes inside for his daily nap and my mum tells me things she can't tell anyone else.

"你的爷爷, 不知道为什么他胆子变的很小。他不想出去也不想一个人呆在家里。他说, '比如有人来敲门, 那我怎么办?' 就想太多呀, 谁会来敲门? 如果他们来敲门, 就不打开门就可以了! 不知道他怕什么。我们家后面住个老太太, 一个人安安静静得

呆着。我就跟他说，你看这个老太太一个人呆在家里没问题，我们就出去一下，你也可以的，你怕什么呢？" | "Your kon-kon, he's gotten really scared recently. I don't know why. He doesn't want to go anywhere, but we can't leave him at home alone, even for a short time. He says, 'But what if someone comes and knocks on the door?' And it's just paranoia—why would someone come and knock on our door? And if they do, all he has to do is not answer it! I don't understand what he's so afraid of! That granny flat behind our house, the old woman lives there alone. So I say to him, 'That old woman behind us lives peacefully and quietly by herself. Why are you so scared about being left home alone?'"

She can't talk to my dad about these things, because they're her parents, not his. As both sets of my grandparents age, the distance is driving a wedge between them. My dad hardly ever gets to see his parents back in China. My parents have been working constantly for over fifteen years and they want a break. They want to go back to China and see what it is like now. But how do they arrange that, with my grandparents being the way they are?

"哎呀我真的没办法，他们也不能照顾自己。我每天会进去看看他们，有时候他们会忘记把炉子关掉，真的好吓人，也许会发生火灾。说实话，他们自己呆在家里我也不太放心。" | "I don't know what to do. They can't look after themselves. I go in from the shop several times a day just to check on them. Sometimes they leave the stove on. I'm so worried. What if they start a fire? Truthfully, I don't feel very safe leaving them at home alone either."

*

When I was in my teens, Kon-kon complained that there were prickles in his eyes. Shards of debris that scraped his eyes as he looked around. This is how that particular habit started, the one where he spends hours in the La-Z-Boy with his eyes closed. It was to avoid the pain. Almost weekly there was an appointment with another doctor or specialist for my mum to ferry my kon-kon to. Finally, he had an operation, and the doctors extracted several growths from the inside of his eye. One was the size of a sunflower seed.

At some point during this process, my mother and Kon-kon discovered a Chinese doctor in Whanganui. My mum came back from an appointment with him and commented to me, "医生说爷爷有 depression."

I had expected to hear more about his eyes, his physical health—anything other than this. The English in her sentence sticks out; there isn't a term in Mandarin for this. I kept my tone neutral and asked, "你懂 depression 是什么意思吗?" | "Do you understand what depression means?"

She repeated some symptoms that the doctor talked about. "Social isolation, no community, lack of activities that would generate a feeling of self-worth." Symptomatic of being the only 崇明人 | Chóngmíngnese in Whanganui. She concluded with a plaintive "没办法。"

Back in Auckland, we knew a few other Chinese families with Shànghǎinese elders. On their walks around Mt Roskill, my grandparents would bump into them. My parents spent three years in Auckland looking for work, but despite their education they could only find jobs as cleaners and factory workers. With two kids and two parents to support, they didn't make enough money to do more than scrape by. So, in 2013, they borrowed money from my dad's family and purchased the combo dairy and fish-and-chip shop. Our family moved down to Whanganui and started our steady trajectory towards the middle class. My parents work seventy-hour weeks with no weekends or holidays. It's not lucrative, but it's not minimum-wage, and they don't have many other choices.

I could see how Mum felt like there wasn't anything they can do for Kon-kon. She seemed to know what depression was, but I wasn't sure if she really understood. It was a word for a Western affliction that required the suffering of an individual family member to be equated with the needs of the family as a whole. I didn't know if she could see past the interdependence that held our family together.

In our family we lack the vocabulary to speak about things that are so delicate, to wade through the overlap in our mutually intelligible language to find the nuance for questions like this.

Once, I asked my bu'uah about the scar on her stomach. It runs the length of her belly and makes all the skin pucker and pull together like a badly folded dumpling.

"Ai-yo ni ge bu'uah ca la le!" | "Aiya . . . your bu'uah is so wretched!" she wailed, rattling off a list of symptoms I didn't understand. It ended with her clenching her right fist, save the thumb, which she drew violently upward along the length of her scar. Her eyes followed the path of the disembowelment, briefly flashing white before she looked back at me.

"Ni kue, ni ge bu'uah ca va?" | "Don't you agree, isn't your bu'uah wretched?"

Technically, my 爷爷奶奶 | grandparents aren't my grand-parents.

My bu'uah adopted my mum when she was two years old. She describes clutching this child, a child she dearly wanted, while my mum screamed at the top of her lungs and pointed down the dirt path. "Ki! Ki! Ki!" | "Go! Go! Go!" she demanded, writing in my bu'uah's arms, urging her to take her back to her biological mother.

My mother was the third girl born into a family that desperately wanted a son. Her birth family couldn't support four children, so they gave her away to my grandparents and tried for a boy child, this time successfully. It was a small village and they were neighbours. They were helping my grandparents out—how wretched it was that my bu'uah couldn't have her own children.

Twenty years later, my mother was one of the few people in Chóngmíng to leave China. And, three years after that, she brought her parents along with her. Her biological family was left behind in rural China.

The first time my mother went back to China was when her biological father died, in 1998. She took me with her. I had no recollection of this grandfather. I didn't know his face, and I didn't yearn to know if I shared it. I remember only snatches of the funeral, gaudy items of red and gold, rice cakes, unknown faces shouting, everything consumed in a smoky fire.

In 2017 my mother's biological mother died. I didn't accompany her to China this time, but I met her for lunch before her flight out of Wellington. I took her to Little Penang, as I didn't think she'd had Malaysian food before. She looked at the unfamiliar menu and asked me to order for her. Knowing our family's tastes, I ordered her a light soup. She ate it with the white porcelain spoon.

I knew nothing about my biological grandmother, not even her name. I wondered if I should feel something about her now, in death. I asked what she had died of, and my mum told me blood poisoning.

"败血症?" | "Blood poisoning?"

"对，她十二年以前得了中风，从那时候开始一直躺在床上，你大姨照顾她，崇明医院也不能送。大姨也不是护士，不懂怎么照顾她。最近她得了褥疮，一直侧着躺，还诱发了败血症。" | "She had a stroke twelve years ago, and has been bedridden ever since. My eldest sister has been looking after her, they don't have access to healthcare in Chóngmíng, you know. She's not a nurse. No one knew how to look after her properly. So she got bed sores from not being turned enough, and that turned to blood poisoning."

I wondered if my mum felt sad about this news, or if she was going to China out of obligation. But there wasn't a way to ask how she felt, not in Mandarin. She continued to speak about how much of a struggle it had been for the entire family to support her mother. The care was a full-time job; it had wrecked her eldest sister financially. Thankfully, the other siblings were in better financial situations and were able to help her out. My mum looked at me seriously. "哎呀 ...... 我希望我一辈子不会给你和你的弟弟那么大的负担。如果我需要机器才能活着，最好就拔掉吧，这也不是什么生活。" | "I hope I'll never be such a burden on you and your brother. If I'm ever on life support, don't hesitate to pull the plug. I wouldn't want to live like that anyway."

"别这样说! 我们在新西兰，这里的医药服务不一样，如果你生病也不会到这么严重的状况。" | "Don't say that! Plus, we're in New Zealand. The level of healthcare is completely different. You'll never get into a state like that."

We continued to eat our food.

I think of my grandparents here, in relatively good health compared with the grandparents left behind. Two years ago, Bu'uah was hit by a car while crossing the road. She waited at the crossing until she saw the green man signalling. She thought it was safe to step out. Stopped at the lights was an elderly woman, anxious to get to her husband in the hospital. She forgot to check for pedestrians as she turned left on the green light. The next day, the headline of the *Whanganui Chronicle* read: "Seventy-year-old woman hits eighty-year-old woman".

My bu'uah's ankle was smashed and needed several screws. The hospital operated on her immediately, and she was wheeled to the same floor as the elderly driver's husband to recover. Her recovery was complicated by her persistent problem with her stomach; she couldn't keep down food and medicines. But she had regular check-ups and rehab, and is back to normal now. Her ankle only feels stiff and sensitive on cold days.

When I moved out of home, my brother got my bedroom. Before that, he'd slept in the same room as my parents. At opposite periods of our lives, my brother and I became only children. I was the only child until I was nine, when my brother was born. Then I left home when he was nine years old, and he became the only child.

My grandparents shared the third bedroom in the house. It had always been too small for the six of us. After I left home, my parents knocked down the carport and built a second living room. It was completed in time for my first visit home from university. I slept in the new living room on a foam mattress.

When I'm home, the three generations of our family eat together. Otherwise, my parents don't often eat with my grandparents. One reason is that my grandparents tend to stir-fry vegetables until they go limp. Neither of them have had their own teeth for at least a decade. Another reason is that they prefer to eat at different times. My grandparents eat early, while my parents fit their dinner around the dinner rush at the shop.

When I'm home, dinner starts just after the takeaways close at 7:30pm. Meal prep begins well before then. Between orders of fish and chips and burgers, my parents fit in chopping, salting, soaking and stewing. There will be at least three different 荤菜 | non-vegetarian dishes. Every night I'm home, it's a feast.

The whole family sits around the table and a bottle of wine is brought out. I can't remember my parents drinking in my childhood, but it's become a regular sight in my last five years of visits.

Tonight there's a lamb leg roast and a whole steamed blue cod. We used to eat their cheaper counterparts, chicken and flounder. My mum carves up the lamb leg. She places a full plate of meat in front of my grandparents, so they don't have to reach. My dad picks up the bone and starts to gnaw, urging my brother and me to have the best cuts of meat. I remember another afternoon chat with my mum in the shop, her remarks on Western family dynamics. How odd it was that the parents bought themselves Magnums but gave cheap Popsicles to their kids. Shouldn't it be the other way around?

I try to tell my bu'uah about my life in Wellington. I tell her that I've started a new job recently. I picked up the Mandarin word for "software developer" when I was last in China, but I don't know how I would say it in Chóngmíng dialect. I simply tell her that I work on a computer.

She nods, seeming to understand. "Ng vi di li gon-zhan yue va?" | "Is your house close to the factory?"

I pause. I say, "Ae, ng ji ja-da-tsheh ki." | "Yes, it's only three kilometres, and I cycle there."

She clucks, laughing at the thought of me choosing to cycle. "Ng ki lar-di mua mi-tsi? Jion-nyng-die 'ai-dzi fu-nyng-die?" |

"Which shop do you shop at, the poor-person shop or the rich-person shop?"

I think of the first time I stepped into Chaffers New World. The fruit was stacked so perfectly. I wondered what my bu'uah would have made of it. Before moving to Wellington, I hadn't set foot in a New World supermarket.

My family was poor, but we were the type of poor that you could work your way out of. I could see it in the way our lifestyle changed. When I entered the professional workforce, I was astonished when my bank balance kept increasing.

I want to tell Bu'uah that I am rich in ways she can't comprehend. It isn't just that I can spend twenty dollars on a meal consisting solely of eggs and bread, or pay for drinks in a bar. I can read and write. I can travel and see the world. I have independence. I have choices.

I know where I shop every week. Partly because it's the closest supermarket to me, but partly because I can.

"Fu-nyng-die," I reply.

# HUSTLE

On Saturdays I go into the office to work on my master's thesis. At home it's too cold and I never get any work done, but at work my desk is set up how I like it and there is an espresso machine. It's quiet but not completely silent, as the call centre still operates over the weekend. Often I see Maneesh from billing in on the weekends too, catching up on work that's flowed over from the week.

Maneesh has a three-litre water bottle with an in-built handle. He got the bottle free when he purchased two tubs of protein powder. He's filling it up when I come into the kitchen.

"How's the thesis going?" he asks.

"Ah, it's going okay. Just a bit tired today."

"Yeah, doing uni and work at the same time is tough, eh, but you gotta hustle."

He looks at me. I know and he knows, and he knows that I know. It's true. Sometimes you have to hustle.

"You know our cleaner is a software developer as well?" he says.

I raise my eyebrows. The cleaner is an Indian man. I see him sometimes when I'm working late. He wears a collared shirt, pressed slacks and a black cap. I wonder if he comes straight from his other workplace, donning the hat on the way.

"Where does he work?" I ask Maneesh.

"Dunno, man, but I think he said he does C++. I was talking to him the other day about it. He works his office job during the day and at night and on the weekends he's got a few cleaning contracts here and at a few other offices."

The cleaner and I nod hello to each other, but we've never stopped to talk.

Maneesh continues, "Yeah, commercial contracts, that's where the money's at in cleaning. You can get it done quickly and businesses don't really mind what you charge them for it. But you know how it is. Us Indians and Asians feel like we gotta play catch-up all the time."

My mum worked as a cleaner when I was in intermediate school. She took out an ad in the community newspaper, and got me to proofread it. It said: "TWO TRUSTWORTHY CHINESE LADIES. FAST AND EFFICIENT CLEANING. $12/HR. PHONE JENNY 093920402".

Jenny is her English name. She changed it because no one could pronounce "Juan", her actual name. Sometimes people would pronounce it "Huan", as in the Spanish form of "John". But 娟 | Juān is pronounced with a soft, curled "j" and flat-toned vowels. It's a common name for Chinese women; it means beautiful or graceful.

So now she was Jenny and she had an ad in the newspaper and another woman who worked with her. One who spoke less English. Mum had found her business associate by putting an ad in one of the Chinese language newspapers.

I didn't need to proofread that one.

Since she was charging twelve dollars an hour, I don't think my mum knew about the ludicrous commercial contracts where she could be paid more for less work. Instead her clients were rich ladies, white, mostly living in Epsom or Remuera. They would phone her up and she'd go to their houses to perform an assessment. Walking from room to room in her Number One Shoe Warehouse sneakers, she would be shown where the vacuum cleaner and ironing board were kept. She would nod, quoting the client a rounded-up number of hours for the work, and scheduling a fortnightly visit.

My dad was in Australia. A family we'd lived with in Rotorua had moved to Melbourne, and their dad had called my dad over to go into business. Together they started an internet café and computer repair shop. Both my parents were running their own businesses. That was typical of Shànghǎinese people. It is said that they have "business acumen". I'm fairly certain, though, that my parents never made much money from either of their ventures. From my mum's descriptions, it sounds like my dad ate away his meagre profits with noodles and yum cha.

Given my parents' work schedules, my grandparents became my primary caregivers. I was old enough to get myself to and from school, and they stayed at home to look after my younger brother, a toddler at the time. Everyone in the family had work to do apart from my brother and me. We were the reason for work.

Once, one of the ladies my mum worked for gave her an Edmonds Cookery Book to give to me. The lady had heard that I enjoyed baking, because I had recently wheedled my mum into buying me a cake tin. The other kids at my school had mums who baked, and I wanted to know what I was missing out on.

I flipped through the cookbook, fascinated by the pancakes, the white sauce, the casseroles. I wanted to make something immediately. But in the baking section most of the recipes had ingredients like vanilla essence, and we didn't keep those in the house.

The next time we went to Pak'nSave I went down the baking aisle, scanning the brightly coloured vials for vanilla essence. There was a range of them and I picked up the one in a smoky plastic bottle marked "Imitation". When I found my mum again, she was in the haircare aisle. She pointed at the Pantene, Sunsilk and Herbal Essence shampoos and conditioners. "The bathrooms I clean always have these brands," she said. "They must be the good ones."

*

I've been working as a software developer since 2012. At my first job, in Christchurch, I worked in a large building with not many windows. I was the only woman in the twenty-person software engineering team. Our office was located in an internal room in the middle of the building. My coworkers wore sneans and Hallensteins polo shirts in navy, black or grey.

There were a handful of people under thirty, and two more women in the wider engineering department. One of the under-thirty testers had gone to an all-boys high school, followed by engineering school, and now he worked five desks away from me. In team meetings he would stare at me. It was like a reflex; he displayed no awareness of his behaviour, or of the fact that I had noticed him doing it.

In my head I'd run through scenarios where I talked to someone about his staring, or about any of the other disorientating interactions I had at work, but I sensed it would be incomprehensible to my manager and my coworkers.

I didn't feel particularly motivated in that job, and I felt isolated because most of my friends had moved to Wellington after graduation to escape post-earthquake Christchurch.

I decided to leave for Wellington too, and was faced with the task of finding a new job. The prospect of staying in the industry wasn't exactly inspiring, but I didn't have relevant experience in any other field. My friends had all struggled with finding employment in Wellington, and I resigned myself to keeping software development open as an option.

I was relieved to find that Wellington had an entirely different tech scene from Christchurch—one of start-ups, social enterprises and striving for gender parity on technical teams. Software development felt newly interesting to me. I started appreciating aspects of it that I hadn't been able to in my old job. I found that I enjoyed turning ideas into something tangible that people could use.

In my current job I have a number of additional responsibilities, including recruitment of software developers. I run the process with my coworker Greg, who I knew before we worked together. We met several years ago through his partner, Serena, who moved to Wellington at around the same time I did.

Serena's parents owned a Four Square in New Plymouth, and were from the same province as the owners of the Dublin Street Dairy in Whanganui. My mum called to notify me that her Dublin Street Dairy friends had friends in New Plymouth who had a daughter around the same age as me. At the time I scoffed at the idea that Serena and I would serendipitously meet in a city as large as Wellington. But a week later we did. The Chinese dairy network foretold it.

When hiring time comes around, Greg and I trawl through the hundreds of CVs and cover letters. We throw out the ones that list the wrong job title or company name. We disregard the ones that start with "Dear Sir". We read through imperfect English to find the intent behind the words. Greg is one of the few coworkers I trust enough to do this exercise with. Most of my colleagues would be able to identify obvious markers of sexism and racism, but they might find it harder to recognise their unconscious biases or microaggressions.

In the holidays Greg went to New Plymouth with Serena. They helped out at the Four Square to give her parents a break. Like my parents, her parents opt to work seventy-hour weeks rather than employ staff. One time, Serena's parents sent Greg back to Wellington with multiple pairs of cargo pants—unsold stock from their failed clothing side-business. So I know that Greg knows about the hustle.

It's important that he knows about the hustle, because every CV we receive from a non-white person reads exactly like my dad's work history. It's hard to dismiss someone when they remind you of someone you know. I can tell that when Greg looks at a CV he sees Serena's father, not some blank face with an unpronounceable name.

*

In China every student takes Mandarin, maths and a foreign language, usually English. Depending on the student's interest, they take additional classes either in social or natural sciences. High school culminates in an intense standardised exam. The exam is commonly referred to as the 高考 | gāokǎo, a simplification of 普通高等学校招生全国统一考试, which means "common university and higher education new students entrance exam taken by the entire country at the same time".

Split over two days, the test is nine hours long and notoriously difficult. The maths section is comparable to university-level maths in Western countries. Essay prompts are indigestible, such as this from the 2018 Shànghǎi paper: "In our daily life, it's necessary to satisfy certain personal needs, but the feeling of being needed by others is also vital, through which we can reflect our self-value. What's your opinion on such universal feeling?"

The entire country holds its breath for these two days. Even the incessant construction pauses. At the gates of the examination halls, parents sit and wait for their children to emerge.

Students are under immense psychological pressure to get good scores in the 高考. For many families, university education is a highly favoured route towards upward mobility, though the university entrance criteria privilege those already living in wealthy areas like Běijīng or Shànghǎi.

In the months leading up to the exam, students spend over twelve hours a day cramming. Studying takes a physical and psychological toll. Many students struggle with anxiety and depression, and every year the examinations and their life-determining results are the reason for a spate of youth suicides.

During the Cultural Revolution there was no 高考. For more than a decade, people wishing to partake in higher education didn't have a clear path to do so. In 1976, the Cultural Revolution ended, and the following year the first 高考 since 1965 was held. It was a historic event, and for that first exam, there was no limit on the applicant's age or education level. The reinstatement of the 高考 by Dēng Xiǎopíng, the vice premier of the People's Republic of China, was widely credited with saving China's educational system, and thus China itself.

Some 5.7 million people sat the 高考 in 1977. Only about 273,000 gained a high enough grade to enter university, which, at 4.8 per cent, was the lowest admission rate in the history of the test. When my dad sat the test in 1980, the same exam paper was given to every student in the country. By then, the university admission rate had increased to 8 per cent. Nowadays, there are plenty of second- and third-tier universities. Most students wishing to go to university can do so; by 2012 the admission rate had risen to 80 per cent.

My 大伯 | uncle once said to me that the only people from Chóngmíng ever to make it to university and out of China were him, my dad and my mum. He's always been one for playful exaggeration, but this particular statement wasn't far from the truth. They each sat the test in different years and were among the lucky few on the island to get high enough scores to go to university in Shànghǎi.

If my dad hadn't got into university, he wouldn't have been able to study engineering. If he hadn't got his degree, he wouldn't have been able to work as an engineer in Shànghǎi and later Guǎngzhōu. If he hadn't worked as an engineer, he wouldn't have had the know-how to chase the capitalist opportunities available in Shēnzhèn when it became a Special Economic Zone. If he hadn't moved to Shēnzhèn, he would never have seen the ad in the newspaper for an emigration service.

My dad is the hustler in the family. My mum would never have instigated something like this, because she didn't share his appetite for risk. The visa application process took over a year and used all of their savings. In 1996 they arrived in New Zealand with three suitcases, a five-year-old child and US$6000 in cash. They knew no one. They had never spoken a word of English in their lives, despite getting a high enough 高考 score in English to be ranked in the top percentile of students. And so, my dad started the hustle again.

*

Greg and I interview an expatriate German man named Dave. A virtual reality start-up in Wellington has run out of investment money and laid off their engineering team; he was one of the technical leads there. At the start of the interview he is quiet, but the conversation picks up quickly. He speaks flawless English.

We've interviewed Daves before: developers who are well known in the community, who have worked at the right places and have plenty of professional regard and social equity. We actively try to sell the job to these people. I tell Dave about the interesting technical challenges and the complexities involved in the work. He nods and asks some insightful questions.

We're frank about what works and what doesn't work in the team. It's about finding a mutual fit. There won't be a scarcity of offers for someone like Dave; he's likely to be talking to several other companies.

We bring him back the next week for a technical interview. His coding style is clear, he is thorough in his explanations, and he can communicate concepts well. Greg and I draw up an offer letter to him with a competitive salary.

Dave declines our offer. He has several offers of equal calibre, and has chosen one of the other ones.

*

As a kid, whenever I asked my parents why we left China, they would reply, "To give you more opportunities." Of course, this wasn't the only factor in our departure. Later I learned that it also had to do with their employment situation. Back then, all companies were state-owned. The factory my mum worked at had been closed down, and she had an indeterminate time to wait until the government issued her a new role.

Meanwhile, my dad was performing well at his job in Shēnzhèn. He had worked his way up and was widely tipped to be the next chairman of the company. But accepting the role would mean an induction to the Chinese Communist Party, as all chairs were political appointments. Leaving the country was a perfect solution for both of these problems. When he told me this story, he said, "我很爱国，可是没那么爱国。" | "I love China, but I didn't love it that much."

During university, my dad was involved with student-led protests and activism. He made light of it, remarking, "当然与学生运动有关联，大部分的人都有关联。大学那时候就是这样的。" | "Of course I protested. Everyone did. It's what you did in university." But five years later the same student-led movement would be massacred in Tiān'ānmén Square. My parents had professed that they were more liberal than most Chinese people, but until I heard that my dad had protested in his youth, I didn't really believe it.

It's hard to say what they believe now. In New Zealand's last general election, my dad voted for National. "穷的时候，我们选了工党。" | "When we were poor, we voted for Labour," he said over dinner. "现在富了，就选国家党。" | "Now that we're rich, we vote for National." At least he was being honest about his self-interest, I supposed. "你肯定会选绿党。" | "You probably vote for the Green Party," he said to me, and mimed smoking a spliff. "他们只关心大麻合法化。" | "All they care about is drug legalisation." That was a rather outdated understanding of the Green Party, so I started talking about their environmental policies, but he cut me off. "你还年轻。长大就会懂了。" | "It's okay, you're young. You'll change your mind when you're older."

For many Chinese people who emigrate, the lack of political empowerment they had in their home country means they are less likely to become politically engaged in their new home.

Add to that the lack of civics education in New Zealand, and the everyday slurs of "Go home", and it makes sense that migrants are one of the largest groups of non-voters in the country.

My mum could easily have been one of these non-voters. She didn't particularly care about politics, and when I lived at home she'd vote for whatever I wanted. For several elections, she was a Greens supporter. When I left home, it was my brother's turn to give guidance. And so, in the 2014 general election, she voted for the Internet Party.

*

Greg and I interview a Chinese man, Xin. His CV indicates that he's had over ten years of experience in the software industry and has worked in international companies with English-speaking teams. We conduct the interview over video conference, as Xin is based in Auckland. The video adds an extra layer of awkwardness to the interview, and Greg and I try to allay that feeling as much as we can.

Xin's speech is stilted and hesitant. I suspect it's the first interview he's had in New Zealand. There's no flow to the conversation; he responds only when asked direct questions. I try to give him opportunities to demonstrate his skills, but other than a few rehearsed answers he doesn't have much to say.

The hour-long interview passes painfully slowly. I know from experience how hard it is to converse in a learned language, let alone give a job interview. But there isn't much I can do other than wait as he formulates his answers. For our last question, we ask him what his future plans are.

"I want to find a job in New Zealand. Then I will bring over my wife and my daughter."

Greg closes the laptop with a sigh. Even though we tried to

work around as many of the barriers as we could, we know we won't be able to create an environment where Xin will succeed. I think of all the failed interviews my dad must have had in New Zealand.

"What can we do?"

"He might have better luck at some of the bigger companies."

"Yeah. I don't think he would work well in a start-up. Somewhere more structured would be better."

I send Xin a rejection email, including recommendations for other places to look for employment. He expresses gratitude for the opportunity to interview. I wonder where he'll end up working, what he'll end up doing. The visa he holds is contingent on his ability to find employment. He's under more pressure than my parents, who were granted residency on arrival.

In China, people often commented on how lucky my family was to leave when we did, what foresight my parents must have had. Since our departure in 1996, immigration controls in New Zealand and other English-speaking countries have tightened significantly. Many people want to leave China, but can't. Just applying for the working holiday visa is competitive, as the website only accepts submissions for a short period of time every year. In this brief window, so many people attempt to apply that the whole website crashes.

The first job that my dad had in New Zealand was at the Agrodome in Rotorua, a tourist trap peddling sanitised sheep farm experiences. He worked as a translator, though later he told me he couldn't understand much of what was being said. He would simply make things up for the Chinese audience and they were none the wiser. In reality, my parents had moved to Rotorua to attend English classes themselves.

Their English lessons must not have changed their employment prospects significantly, as our family's next shift was to Palmerston North so that my dad could go to the university there, Massey, and gain his master's degree in mechanical engineering. He spent two years modelling the fluid mechanics of coolant through the packaging for apples.

Despite his work experience and the prestige of having gained university entrance in China, none of that mattered as much as the piece of paper from Massey University. He finally landed an engineering job and our family moved again, this time to South Auckland. It was an entry-level role in a factory, and the salary was barely enough to support our family now that my brother had been born. Dad realised that it would be hard for him to work up the ladder as he had done in China. New Zealand had a different work culture, and there wasn't anyone who could show him the new rules. So he tried to go into business—first with the internet café in Melbourne, and later the dairy in Whanganui, borrowing money from family to buy it.

I can see why my dad didn't last long at the one professional job he had in Aotearoa. So much of what he needed to relearn was tied to language ability, which was never a strength of his. He spent two years working in Guǎngzhōu and didn't learn to speak a word of Cantonese.

In Whanganui my parents have a small Chinese community of four or five families. They aren't the only Chinese people in the city, but they have gravitated towards one another through shared circumstance. They all migrated to New Zealand at around the same time, have master's or doctorate degrees, and currently spend their days selling dollar mixtures. They pass their aspirations for higher-paid work on to the next generation. Within this community, parents would prefer their children to become doctors, lawyers, engineers or accountants.

I grew up understanding the necessity of work and expecting a certain degree of meniality. We didn't talk about following your passion, or the idea that work might provide anything other than material fulfilment. My parents worked because they had to, but in Wellington I became aware that people around me derived some sort of personal meaning from their jobs. I thought of the doctors, lawyers, engineers and accountants that I knew and wondered how they would feel about moving to the regions and having my parents' job: the thirteen-hour days, the burger-flipping, the danger of robbery.

Once, I posed this question of job satisfaction to my dad. He shrugged, scraping the grill clean with the fish slice. "有时候通过所有的流程不现实。" | "Sometimes it's not practical to retrain," he said, speaking of our family friends who were doctors in China but acupuncturists in New Zealand. Out came the catering spread, lettuce and tomato from the fridge. "有时候不想从事以前的工作。" | "Some never wanted to continue their careers in New Zealand," he said, speaking of the Gāos, who were university professors of architecture in China. The fish was lifted, golden yellow, out of the fryer. "我忽然想到，高阿姨卖掉了他们的咖啡店，现在在建筑公司上班。" | "Actually, I just remembered Aunty Gāo recently sold their café and is now working for an architecture firm in town." The burger was placed in a paper bag and my dad upended the bag to twist it closed.

He motioned to the waiting customer. "Best fish burgers in town!" the customer exclaimed as he reached over the counter for the package.

My dad gave a toothy grin. "Good!"

*

45

Greg and I interview a woman from the Philippines, Hazel. We've had hundreds of people apply for the developer role, but just two of them are women. After the CV review, we're left with only Hazel making it to the interview stage.

No meeting rooms are free, so we arrange to meet at a coffee shop across the street. Greg and I arrive early and offer Hazel a coffee upon her arrival. She declines. She seems nervous. She tells us she has spent a few months applying for jobs and has had no success. When she answers our questions there's a waver in her voice, and her palms repeatedly rub the fabric of her pants.

We learn that Hazel moved to New Zealand with her German partner, who had a job lined up before they left Malaysia. In Malaysia she worked for a large telecommunications company. Her previous work was more akin to network programming, and she's aware that her skills have lagged behind the current technologies. But we can see that she's determined. She's moved from the Philippines to Malaysia and then to New Zealand. Adapting to new technologies will be a breeze.

We'd scheduled a technical interview with Hazel, but she isn't familiar with either of the two programming languages that we offer the assessment in. She last worked in Perl. It would be a disadvantage to assess her against something she doesn't know, so Greg spent the evening rewriting the assessment in Perl. Being responsible for hiring has been a disillusioning reminder of how homogenous the industry is, and we clutch at any opportunity to level the playing field.

Hazel is hired and she starts immediately. Greg and I rearrange desks so that the three of us can sit in the same cluster. In her first three months Hazel focusses on learning Ruby. She tilts her head towards us whenever she has a question. Greg and I improve our team processes from her feedback and decide that we could hire some junior developers. After we recruit these new team members, Greg decides to step back from hiring. But our team needs to expand by at least five more developers, so more people need to be involved in interviewing. Greg and I consider the suitability of our coworkers, and extend some invitations. One of them is to Hazel.

I pitch the idea to her and she looks terrified. She has been at the company for half a year now, but it's only been in the last month that she's felt comfortable talking in front of a group of more than four people. Hazel tells me that she knows that she has to do the things she finds the hardest, and for that reason she accepts the invitation. She tells me that when Greg and I interviewed her she was perplexed that it was held in a coffee shop. "I wasn't sure if I was allowed to have a coffee," she says. Surely drinking coffee wasn't formal enough? She'd had no idea what to expect or how to behave.

Hazel often comes to me with queries about the idiosyncrasies of New Zealand life. I tell her that she can write "Return to Sender" on envelopes to post back letters that were addressed to the previous occupants of their flat. When the weather appears to thaw after winter, I warn her not to expect the fine spell to last for long.

The next round of recruitment attracts even more applications than last time, and we decide that it would be better to split the workload. Each hiring committee member pairs up with another developer on the tech team to conduct the interviews.

Because there are so many applicants, it's impossible for everyone to meet them all. In those cases we trust the judgement of our peers. At the end of the process, four people accept job offers.

One lunchtime Hazel and I are heating up our leftovers in

the kitchen. She has pan-fried fish on rice, I have stir-fried pork and garlic shoots on rice. We sit at the table and I ask her about the van she's fitting out with her partner.

"Oh, it's so much work. Every weekend we're working on the van. And so expensive! All the tools are expensive here!"

They're trying to get the van finished by summer so they can travel around New Zealand. We fall into silence for a while.

Then Hazel says, "Can I ask you a question about the culture here?"

"Sure, of course."

"You know I don't have many people to ask, and I don't want to get anything wrong."

"Yeah, it's hard learning a new culture."

"I just don't want to offend anyone."

"Of course. You can ask me all the stupid questions you want." I'm curious what she wants to ask. It isn't like her to be this bashful.

"The new developer we hired—Kelsey."

"Oh, sure."

"You said she was a . . . tr . . ."

"Trans woman?"

"Yeah, trans woman. What does that mean?"

After Kelsey's interview, I had felt conflicted about whether to tell the rest of the hiring committee about her gender identity. She had brought it up of her own accord, so I assumed she wanted us all to know, but it had felt weird to talk about her when she wasn't in the room. It was one of the reasons she was looking for another job. Her previous job was unsupportive and unresponsive to questions of culture and identity, as well as having incredibly long hours.

When the committee got together to talk about Kelsey, one coworker had said, "I thought it was weird that she said she

48

didn't care what tech stack she was working in, but just wanted a good team."

"I can understand that," I replied. "I felt the same in my first job out of uni. I hated the culture there so much, it was either find a better team or leave the industry entirely. It didn't matter what I was doing."

"Okay, that makes sense."

"It sounded like there was a lot about her old job's culture that didn't work for her."

"Yeah, she said she was trans, eh? That would be hard."

I think of my workplace as being fairly progressive, but it's hard to know people's values until they're put into situations that expose them. I was relieved when we moved on to Kelsey's technical skills. It would have been disingenuous to offer her a better work environment if that hadn't been confirmed by the behaviour of my coworkers.

I've worked with a few trans women in a previous job. Before then, I had understood and accepted what being trans meant on an intellectual level. But I was nervous when I had to put that into practice. I had the same fear as Hazel of inadvertently saying the wrong thing. I became more aware of my language. I found resources to read.

Over our lunches, I help Hazel understand the basics of transgender identity. It isn't something I have expertise in, but I know enough to allay Hazel's worries about inadvertently offending our new coworker.

"In the Philippines, we don't talk about this stuff," she says. I realise I know nothing about the Philippines, or their queer community.

"I try to look it up, but it's so hard," she continues. "My English reading is so slow and it's hard to know what is a good source."

"Yeah. It's hard to filter information that isn't in your native language."

"Yes, so hard! It's much easier to talk to someone who's from the culture themselves. Then you know that it's right."

*

The houses around my family's dairy are brick or weatherboard, with stingy windows. It's mostly state housing and pensioners' flats. "每周四店很忙因为这一天政府发 benefit." | "The shop is always busy on Thursdays because benefit payments have come through," my mum says. My parents aren't sympathetic to the cycle of poverty, even though they've been in it themselves. Because they have broken out of it, they think others should be able to as well, despite the different circumstances people face in China and New Zealand.

My dad is dismissive of New Zealand history. They haven't been exposed to much of it, apart from the "settler" narrative foregrounded in mainstream media. "比不上中国上下五千年的历史。" | "It's nothing compared to the five-thousand-year history of China," he says, a belief often voiced by Hàn Chinese people. In that story, we were the dominant majority. Our Hàn ancestors colonised neighbouring regions to expand borders into what is now recognised as modern China. Under the banner of unification, they homogenised the other fifty-five recognised ethnic groups of China. Given this background, I don't know how my parents would view the theft and brutality that "New Zealand" was built upon.

For a long time my parents paid rent on the house and dairy to their Pākehā landlords, the previous shop owners. After some persuasion, my parents have been able to buy the commercial property from them. Now they are the landlords. The dairy has been sold to another Chinese couple in Whanganui, and the rental income is enough for my parents to live on. I can't begrudge them for their hustle. It has relieved them of the tiring work and given a younger couple stable work in a town that's low in employment opportunities.

I have lunch with Greg and Serena and tell them about my parents' retirement. They know the dairy life well. In a blog post about going back to her parents' Four Square in New Plymouth for Lunar New Year, Serena wrote about how the store didn't get many customers. The supermarkets were cheaper, and no one had much money to spend.

Serena shares the same outlook on our parents' work situations as I do. Of the people I tell about my parents' retirement, she's the only one who grasps the significance of the situation.

"How did they manage to do that?" she asks.

"They bought the property off the old owners, and now they're living on rent money."

Serena pauses, then says, "My parents tried to do that too. But the owners backed out. I don't know what they can do now, but I want them to be able to stop working."

Her parents are overqualified for what they're doing, like mine were. "That sucks," I say.

Serena shrugs in acknowledgement. Sometimes the hustle only gets you so far.

# 剔骨刀 | CLEAVER

The cleaver is a flash of stainless steel. The blade is rectangular, about 25 centimetres in length and almost a centimetre thick at the spine. The tang runs the full length of the handle, which is a flattened cylinder of metal with the same brushed hue. Two grooves on the bottom edge of the handle blend seamlessly with its sides. The curves and lines of the cleaver have an ease to them, a fluidity, as if metal naturally flows into these shapes. Just looking at the heavy blade makes me quiver. It can part meat and bone with one strike. My fingers twitch with the urge to take the handle and close my grip around its perfectly shaped bottom edge. It'll have a good heft to it. The blade is stamped with the logo of its manufacturer, 广东阳江特珠钢 | Guǎngdōng Yángjiāng Special Steel.

Using a cleaver is about force and momentum. My dad brings the cleaver upward and lets it swing down under its own weight. *Bang!* A fish's head is severed from its body, jaw shuddering from the impact. My dad turns the cleaver, calling its flat surface into action. *Smack!* A thumb of ginger splatters open, spilling its aroma. My dad rocks the cleaver back and forth on the chopping board. *Fwup! Fwup! Fwup!* A spring onion stalk is slashed into four segments. My dad faces the blunt spine of the cleaver down. *Thump! Thump! Thump!* A cucumber is crushed, white seeds and clear fluid flowing out of its jagged surface.

Using a cleaver requires precision. *Tap-a-tap-a-tap-a-tap!* My dad finely dices cloves of garlic into pointed tips. *Thump. Thump. Thump.* The cleaver passes through a hunk of aromatic braised beef, slices falling cleanly and evenly. With a cupped hand at one end of the meat and the cleaver at the other, my dad runs the cleaver along the chopping board, scooping slices of meat onto its flat edge.

There is a Chinese proverb that goes "好肉长在骨头边", meaning "The best meat is next to the bone". Sweet-and-sour spare ribs, a dish originating from the Shànghǎi region, has always been a favourite in our family. The pork ribs need to be cut into one-inch segments, perfect mouth-sized morsels. My dad is well practised with the cleaver. *Bang! Bang! Bang!* He lifts it to chest-height and still the blows land exactly where he intends.

Often I'll see him sitting on the step outside the kitchen, holding the cleaver in one hand and a whetstone in the other. The whetstone is soaked in water for an hour before it is used. When it's ready, the matte stone has the same texture as the black sand shore at Kai Iwi after a wave has receded. My dad passes the length of the cleaver along the whetstone in one steady stroke. The contact makes a soothing sound, like a branch dragged across concrete. He turns the cleaver over. The sharpened side catches the light. He draws the underside along the coarse stone, and the sun's reflection dances on its bevelled edge.

Every couple of years, the cleaver is replaced by an identical successor. The cleavers we buy can withstand only so much sharpening and split only so much bone before their cutting edge is too thin and jagged to be useful. The old cleaver is retired from the kitchen. My bu'uah takes it for her garden. She chops the lawn with it, turning over the grass to clear a vegetable patch.

Western-style knives typically have a wedge-shaped blade. Compared with Chinese knives, they are smaller and lighter with much thinner blades. Depending on the intended purpose of the Western knife, it has a variety of grinds—hollow, convex and compound to name a few. For this reason, a Western kitchen has numerous knives with different grinds and forms. A Chinese kitchen often has just one: the flat-ground cleaver. Sometimes there is a secondary 菜刀 | vegetable knife, also with a wide rectangular blade. Outsiders often mistakenly identify it as a cleaver, as it has the same profile, but the blade is not heavy or thick enough to cut through bone. Hence the Mandarin for cleaver is 剁骨刀 | bone-chopping knife.

Even professional Chinese chefs prepare ingredients with just their cleaver. Careful attention is paid to how things are cut, as this influences the flavour and texture of the dish. If you want to say that a blade is sharp, in Mandarin you say that it is 快 | quick. I have watched an experienced chef slice tofu into hair-thin strands, light enough to float to the top of a bowl of soup. "Quick" seems to me a much better characterisation of the knife's power.

As Chinese food is eaten with chopsticks, all of the chopping is done during the preparation of the dish. There are many ways to shape the ingredients.

段 means segments, like snapping off sections of young bamboo shoots.

片 means thin slices, like peeling rounds from a crisp carrot.

块 means chunks, like carving a potato into smaller blocks.

丁 means small cubes, like dicing a cucumber into fingertip-sized portions.

条 means strips, like turning a sheet of tofu skin into wide noodles.

丝 means thin strips, like shredding a turnip so finely that it is akin to silk.

末 means powder, like mincing garlic until it turns to fresh snow.

There are also many ways to feel the cleaver's striking action.

斩 means to behead, to dismember the animal while it is still alive. This is how freshness is ensured.

剁 means to chop, but with a speed, a vigour to it. The fast pitter-patter sound of the cleaver needs to be heard.

砍 means to hack, to use a large sweeping motion to engage the full power of the metal. The same word is used to describe the force to fell trees.

切 means simply to cut, to use the cleaver as you know how.

There is a Chinese dish from the Yángzhōu region called 三套鸭 | three-nested ducks. The dish consists of three birds—a pigeon, a domestic duck and a wild duck—nested within one another.

I once watched a video of a chef preparing this elaborate dish. He fans the three birds out in front of him. They are plucked and gutted, wholly intact except for an incision at the base of their necks. The chef explains that the birds need to be deboned, but the skin must remain unperforated. He reaches for the neck of the wild duck with one hand, cleaver ready in the other. The cleaver widens the incision at the duck's throat to meet the shoulder. The chef begins to meticulously turn the bird inside out, extracting the bones of the ribcage, then the wings and the legs. He is careful not to tear any of the skin in this process, especially the delicate section around the duck's chest.

The resulting carcass looks like a deflated rubber duck, but as he says, the shape of the duck is retained. It is vital to the success of the dish that the shape of the duck is retained. The pigeon is nested within the domestic duck, and the domestic duck is nested within the wild duck. The body of the wild duck is now filled out to the plumpness of a healthy bird. Three bird heads stick out of the wild duck's body, curving together like a set of spoons.

I flirted with the idea of making this dish, and found a recipe online. The opening line was "将家鸭、野鸭和鸽子宰杀治净", translating as "First slaughter the domestic duck, wild duck and pigeon cleanly".

When I was ten, my kon-kon got his hands on a live chicken. It was reddish-brown, a retired laying hen. Even though chicken meat could easily be purchased, my kon-kon had an urge to prepare chicken soup the traditional way.

He slaughtered it right there, in the backyard of our house in Panmure. I couldn't see, or didn't look, at the moment the cleaver came down on the chicken's neck.

*

Tom and I slow our pace on the bicycles, peering at the restaurants set up on the side of the road. The proprietors sense the opportunity for a sale and beckon us, calling, "美女! 来吃饭!" We stop at a restaurant with tables outside. An awning shields us from the heavy sun, but we can still look out to the karst mountains that line the horizon.

The 老板娘 | owner walks over and hands us a laminated menu. "试下啤酒鱼吧。" | "Try the beer fish," she says, pointing to the local specialty. 啤酒鱼 | Beer fish is made with live carp from 漓江 | the Lí River, which runs through the north-east of the 广西 | Guǎngxī region. The river passes through 阳朔 | Yángshuò, where we sit for lunch.

To prepare the dish, the carp is gutted and split in half, but left unscaled. Seasonings are rubbed onto the fish before it is tossed into a roaring pot of oil. As the scales cook, they soften but keep a firm hold of the flesh underneath, contracting, curling and changing to a wan yellow. As soon as the colour changes, the fish is lifted out of the fryer and doused with soy sauce. Braising completes the process, preferably with water from 漓江 | the Lí River and beer from the 广西 | Guǎngxī region. Tomatoes and chilli are added.

We had the dish for dinner yesterday but we're happy to order it again. After all, it calls for fish and beer from this location, and we aren't likely to be here again soon. We're hungry so I add two vegetable dishes to our order and deliberate on one more.

There's a section for 土鸡 | organic chicken. The birds are priced by weight and served however you like—poached, fried, turned into broth. Since we've already ordered an entire fish, I wonder if a portion of chicken would be too much.

"可以买一斤鸡吗?" I ask the owner.

"最少一斤半。"

"那不点了, 我们只是两个人, 怕吃不下。"

"一斤半只是半个鸡, 分量是从活鸡算的, 包括内脏、鸡毛。处理好差不多一斤, 两人吃可以的。"

"好, 点个白斩鸡。"

I explain to Tom that I've ordered half a chicken. It's about a kilo but the weight calculation includes the feathers and the guts, so when the dish arrives the portion will only be about 500 grams. Manageable for us to eat. He nods. The owner heads back to the kitchen, shouting our order ahead of her.

We watch a puppy with coarse, sandy hair trot across the road and scamper into a field of crops. The owner walks past our table and follows the path of the puppy across the road and down the bank, slipping out of view. I see snatches of her head as she walks further out, then she disappears behind a curtain of green vegetation.

A rooster crows absently. The mountains ahead form irregular peaks, shorter and narrower than the hills I am familiar with. Patches of grey and white limestone peek out from a thicket of dense bush. The owner is crossing the street again now. When she reaches our table she raises her right arm slightly, showing us her grasp around the ankles of a rooster. He hangs limply from clawed feet, belly facing us. The patch around the rooster's navel, or where it would be if roosters had navels, is shiny pink and bare of downy feathers. I don't know if this is normal; I've never seen a rooster from this angle. I spot the familiar curve of a drumstick, and follow my eyes down his floppy neck to his red wattled head, swaying slightly as he hangs upside down.

Seeing that we are satisfied, the owner takes the rooster back to the kitchen.

Tom looks at me, and shrugs. "I thought the 'feathers and guts' was a metaphor, but okay."

The last time I saw a dead chicken, it was neatly plucked, gutted and beheaded. I bought it for twelve New Zealand dollars. Without all the mess, it weighed in at one and a half kilograms.

In English, we prefer to disguise our consumption of meat

with euphemisms. Pork, beef, mutton. In Mandarin, the words for animal meat are precisely that: the character for the animal, followed by the character for meat. 猪肉、牛肉、羊肉。 It is hypocritical not to acknowledge that meat comes from animals, and impossible not to be confronted with it in Chinese cooking, where all parts of the animal are eaten. Pig's skin is boiled to make the delicious soup in 小笼包 | soup dumplings; duck blood is a hot pot specialty. Everything is served as it is, with the bones, with the head, with the knowledge that you are eating something that was alive, perhaps just moments before.

Dishes come out as they're ready. First is the fish, followed by the vegetables. The rooster is the last to come, but it hasn't felt like we've been waiting very long, given the amount of preparation needed.

The plated-up half-rooster is smaller than a bird back home, and has thicker and yellower skin. No wonder. The rooster was a fully grown bird, plucky and orange, moments ago strutting around with its neck bobbing back and forth.

It wasn't a white-feathered broiler chicken, the only variety available to farm commercially in New Zealand. Broilers are cultivated to have a relentless manner of feeding; to convert efficiently from grain to mass. They live in cramped containers, eating and shitting on the same floor. Their legs and feet are burned by ammonia from the layers of excrement. These burns don't look appetising, and are removed by butchers.

On an ordinary chicken farm, broilers are killed at thirty-eight days; on an organic farm they make it to eight to ten weeks. But even when these chickens are rescued from slaughter, they don't live past a year. They die of size-related issues. They get so big so fast that their hips fail to support them. Incapable of walking and unable to stop eating, they gorge until they die.

A friend once recounted some banter he had with a Tegel chicken farmer in the communal kitchen of a campground near Nelson. "When the first chickens start dying of heart attacks, that's when you know the flock is about ready."

*

Before I left home for university I asked my mum how she learned to cook. She said she observed her parents and picked it up. I was sceptical. How was it possible to learn just by watching? What information could we absorb unconsciously without going through the motions ourselves? As a parting gift, my mum gave me a rice cooker.

In my undergraduate years my flatmates and I had a cooking roster and we bought food communally. Meat came in bulk packs. Black styrofoam trays were snapped into two or three, slimy soakers discarded and individual portions sealed and frozen. The vegetable selection at the Western supermarket was dull, and we bought the same things every time.

The closest approximation of Chinese food that my flatmates made was stir-fry, or fried rice. But the flavours were wrong. Where was the Chinese sausage, and why was there sweet soy sauce? One flatmate was baffled that I used the rice cooker for rice. "But can't you just use a saucepan?" she said as she put bread in the toaster. "Why would you have an entire appliance that did just one thing?"

Later, I lived in houses where cooking was no longer shared, and I had the money to buy the ingredients that I wanted. I bought dried fragrant mushrooms, green soybeans, lotus root, wood ear and pressed tofu at the Chinese supermarket. My rice cooker broke and I bought a new one. I set about cooking dishes the way I remembered them, guided by the details I recalled from my parents' kitchen. Strips of peeled eggplant soaking in the kitchen sink. Three cuts along the side of the whole snapper. Dumplings brought to the boil three times, skin puffy and milky.

Tom was already an accomplished cook when we met. He liked Middle Eastern cuisine and introduced me to ingredients like dried limes and sumac. But now he wants to learn to cook Chinese food, because he knows that's the only thing that will truly impress me and my family. One evening I instruct him to chop up some 大白菜 | Chinese cabbage for a stir-fry. I trust that he knows what he's doing, so I attend to the 红烧肉 | braised pork I have on the stove. When I turn back around I scream. He's chopped the cabbage the wrong way—separating the crinkly green leaves from the white stems. I can't articulate why it's wrong, but I know that it is. Moments like this happen time and again, and I realise the breadth of knowledge I've picked up in my parents' kitchen.

Tom and I go to Whanganui and hover while my dad cooks. He chops pork into thin slices and tosses them into the hot wok. My bu'uah has prepared a colander of flat beans. They're from her garden, and have been washed, dethreaded and snapped into thumb-length segments. Dad picks one up and waves it at us. "必须把那根筋摘掉，否则不好吃。" | "You must dethread them, or else it won't be tasty." He turns the pork a couple of times, then adds the beans, soy sauce, cooking wine, a cup of water and a little bit of sugar.

He places a lid on the wok, muffling the low rumbling sound. My dad has already par-boiled the noodles, but he grabs the packet from the cupboard to show me. "这就是你们那边 Yan's 买到的。" | "These were purchased at your local, Yan's." My glasses mist as he lifts the lid. He scoops out half of the stew's liquid into a bowl. "这是一个很重要的步骤，你们好好看。" | "This is an important step, watch closely." The tangle of noodles is arranged over the stewing beans and meat, and the lid is replaced. "让它焖一下。" | "Let it stew for a while." A few minutes later, he lifts the lid again. The noodles are visibly softer, collapsed and wilting on the bed of vegetables. He pours half the bowl of liquid over the noodles and replaces the lid. "这样煮面就好吃了。" | "If you cook it like this, the noodles will be tasty." One more round of liquid on the noodles, then the vegetables and meat are mixed through.

My dad serves up the bowls of noodles and we take them to the table. The noodles and pork are a light tan colour. The beans are still bright. We eat in silence, engrossed in the food. The only sound is of noodles being sucked into mouths.

In Chinese recipes, the quantities for seasonings—salt, soy sauce, garlic—are given as 适用, or "as applicable". The recipe relies on the accuracy of the cook's tongue to know what the dish should taste like. If you prefer saltier, more strongly flavoured food, it is said that your palate is "heavier". Shànghǎinese palates are said to be 清淡, or "light". The flavours of our region are delicate with a touch of sweetness.

Mandarin has an expansive vocabulary for taste. Spicy food is popular in many regions, and each region has a specialised word for their distinct flavour of spice. Numbing spice. Oily spice. Fragrant spice. And there are words for the way that food interacts with the rest of the mouth, not just the taste buds. It's important to consider the 口感 | mouth feel. Is it slippery or smooth? Does it have elasticity, or does it crumble?

Tom starts researching Chinese recipes. He finds a few good English-language blogs, and uses Google Translate for the ones on 下厨房 | Xiàchúfáng, a popular website for Mandarin-language recipes. The conversion gives the recipes a lyrical quality: "I had an eagerness to open the fire / and the wood had noticed / that the soup had dried up."

He discovers recipes outside the regions I'm familiar with, and challenges the intuitions that I hold about the shape and composition of Chinese food. One recipe pairs spinach and peanut, two things I wouldn't have thought to put together. The dish is popular in the Northeast, far from the southern cuisine of my home.

Soon, the tools Tom and I have at home need to be upgraded to match our growing abilities. We decide to buy a cleaver. Our local Chinese supermarket has none in stock, so we go to a knife wholesaler in the city. They only have one cleaver in stock. Unlike the cleaver in my parent's kitchen, the tang is not straight. It curves upward, and has a round hole for hanging the knife on a meat hook or a butcher's belt. The cleaver is not considered standard equipment for most home cooks.

To test out the cleaver I decide to make 白斩鸡 | white cut chicken, a Cantonese recipe. The chicken flesh needs to be juicy and succulent, and to achieve this the chicken is poached for twenty minutes then left in the broth for two hours to soak. After it is lifted out of the pot it is doused in ice water to shrink the skin so that it clings tightly to the flesh. The skin is patted dry and rubbed with sesame oil. Once it has cooled completely, it can be cut and served.

I start the recipe in the afternoon. My first struggle is to lift the bird out of the pot. I consider pouring it into a colander, but it seems like a waste of perfectly good chicken stock. The bird is too hot and oily for me to get a good grasp on it. The drumsticks seem like a good place to pull, but the meat is so soft the legs start to separate from the body, tearing the delicate skin at the thigh. I managed to get it out eventually, with its legs gaping only slightly outward.

Sharon arrives for dinner just as I'm about to make the first cleave. Like me, she is familiar with cleavers from her parents' kitchen. She and Tom watch from a safe distance as I pick up the cleaver. Looking at the chicken, I try to recall the times I watched my mum cut up a roast duck—first, she would halve the bird by cutting down one side of the spine. I place the cleaver along the length of the ribcage, and press gingerly. The blade is so heavy that the bones crumple like paper, exposing an inside view of the spine. I adjust the cleaver again. In one rocking motion, I chop alongside the spine and the bird is in two pieces. Using the knife is delightful. I grin at Sharon and Tom.

Next I cut along the hip joints, taking off the thighs and drumsticks. The first side separates easy. *Fwoop!* The other side is much harder, and I realise I haven't quite found the joint, the easy path to cut along. *Crunch!* I plough through splintery bone rather than soft cartilage. Breast next. I aim to chop three-inch-thick portions of meat, but the pieces end up irregular and uneven.

A gritty residue of blood, marrow and bone is along the cutting edge of the cleaver. With dismay, I notice that the inside of the chicken breast is pink. Too pink.

"Oh no!" I say, holding up a piece to show Sharon and Tom. "Do you think it's too undercooked?"

Sharon looks closely. "Yeah, maybe . . . You could just put it in the microwave for a while. That's what my dad does if he's undercooked it."

Into the microwave it goes. I serve it up, feeling slightly deflated. But I still send a photo to our family WeChat group. My dad replies:

看上去很美, 有一点馋

# HOW IS YOUR HEALTH?

"With my yoga I feel like I'm getting younger every day!" Sylvia says while demonstrating a handstand to the class. We're in her garage, which she's renovated as a studio with full-length mirrors on one side and ballet-style barres on the other. Her feet occasionally flutter away from the support of the wall behind her. "Next year, Rose and I are both going to turn twenty-five!" I'm twenty-four and Sylvia is seventy-two.

Sylvia calls postures by their traditional Sanskrit names, which I will later learn is typical of Iyengar teachers. She instructs the class to set up for Sarvangasana. I don't know the Sanskrit names, so I wait to see what everyone else is doing. Following the other students' lead, I lie on a pile of woollen blankets then kick my legs up over my head, creasing my body like an origami mountain fold. We raise one leg then the other into the air, supported by our arms folded at the elbow like brackets, and hands on the small of the back.

"Sarvangasana is the queen of all asanas," Sylvia says. She is marching around the room, appraising our postures, making sure our legs stand up straight like marble pillars. "Your knees and your feet should be together!" she says when it's my turn. I close the small gap between my knees, but I struggle to bring my ankles any closer. The bulk of my thighs is in the way. I can't do it. My legs feel like they're on fire and there's still at least a ten-centimetre gap between them.

"Sylvia, I don't think it's physically possible," I say, watching beads of sweat form on my kneecaps. I haven't seen my knees sweat since I stopped doing hot yoga. I didn't realise it was possible to sweat like this in an unheated room.

"Of course it is!" she barks. She hits my right thigh. "These legs are all bulk! They're not working! I want to see them working!" My thighs clench tighter and I feel like I've broken through a barrier. "That's better! Now keep them like that! Over time your legs will change and they will come together!" Satisfied, Sylvia walks away. My ankles aren't any closer. I look at my right thigh. It starts shaking from exertion.

After what feels like an eternity, we exit the pose. I lie on my back, legs quivering. On the mat next to me is Terry, Sylvia's partner. As a way of apologising for Sylvia's behaviour, he leans over and tells me that she used to be a gymnastics coach. "Hitting provokes an instant response from the muscles. She's used to doing that type of coaching, where you have to get them to just do it."

After class, Sylvia tells me about her coaching career. Her daughter Fiona was one of the top gymnasts in England. "You would have made a good gymnast too. You've got the build for it. Short, stocky thighs, flexible." She's taken an interest in me, inquiring about other forms of exercise I do and where I normally practise in Wellington.

I tell her I have been practising yoga at least twice a week for the last three years. I thought I had gotten pretty good. But this class made me feel like a beginner. It wasn't that the poses she taught were more challenging; it was that she demanded an exact level of precision of every posture. Under her instruction, even the most basic postures became difficult again.

She imparts to me that not all styles of yoga are the same. She *psshes* at all the yoga styles I've done in the past. "*Pssh*, power vinyasa, *pssh*, hot yoga. *Pssh!* They're all rubbish! You don't learn anything in those classes. You need to be doing Iyengar." The corners of her mouth are wet with spittle. Her hands are on her hips and she tilts her head up at me, her posture perfect. Though she's scarcely five feet tall and under fifty kilos, she isn't someone to be argued with.

The next morning when I wake up, I'm the sorest I've ever been after a yoga class. I'm hooked on this Iyengar thing. I head back to her studio again the next day.

I'm sorry to be leaving Havelock North that afternoon and heading back to Wellington. "Come back any time," she tells me. "You can stay with Terry and me and do yoga."

*

Every time I went home during the university holidays, my mum would weigh me. It feels wrong to talk about this in English. "Fat" has different connotations in Mandarin. While fatness is still considered undesirable, the word can also be used more neutrally, as a descriptor of appearance. Someone can be tall. Someone can have brown hair. And that someone can also be fat.

My mum weighed me out of interest, to check that nothing had drastically changed since the last time she saw me. If my weight had changed significantly, she'd comment on it in the same way you'd comment on your neighbour's house if they had painted it a different colour. Irrespective of any weight change, she would then ask how many dumplings I wanted to eat for lunch. "只吃二十个? 不够吧。你该吃二十五个吧, 跟你弟弟一样。" | "Oh, only twenty? Not enough. You should eat twenty-five, that's how many your brother has."

In China, my dad was fat. His fatness was well known and well regarded in their hometown. He was respectably fat. My aunt once commented to me, "我们陆家人都长得圆圆的。" | "Us Lùs—round faces, fat bodies." I come from a line that is stocky, with wide frames and thick thighs. Our bodies are purposeful, like bricks.

When my parents arrived in New Zealand, my dad realised he had lost his signature largeness. By New Zealand standards he was a medium at best. The different diet was to blame. People here grew up pleasantly plump on their diet of milk and honey. He could never catch up.

Here, fatness is seen differently. I told my Pākehā flatmates about my family's ceremonial weighing, instigated by my arrival back home but incorporating all family members. My flatmates responded in horror, and I had to backtrack to explain the joy of the situation. The weighing often caused us to break into hysterics, especially as my brother grew older and crept up in the family weight rankings to challenge our father for the top spot. My family's no-nonsense way of talking about bodies isn't quite normalised in New Zealand.

My grandma often talks about her constipation until I recommend she drink alpine tea. After a particularly spicy meal my dad asks if anyone else has diarrhoea. On the phone we ask each other, "你的身体怎么样?" | "How is your health?", a greeting grounded in an inquiry of wellbeing.

*

Sylvia emails me from the Xtra account she shares with Terry. She's covering for a teacher in Wellington and invites me to attend the weekend workshop she's holding. I head along to the studio with my girlfriend Jade.

As in Sylvia's Havelock North classes, Jade and I are decades younger than the other students. I had thought that this was due to the demographics of the area, but it seems that Iyengar practitioners tend to be older. I don't know what the regular students of this Wellington studio are more surprised by: the appearance of youngsters, or Sylvia's approach to teaching.

"Come on, you lot!" Sylvia says by way of encouragement. From the corner of my eye I see a face twitch involuntarily.

We're doing arm variations but not getting into them fast enough. Garudasana is next, where forearms and hands are intertwined.

Sylvia casts an eye over the room, stopping at Jade. "Gosh, you've got arms like the Hulk!"

Jade grimaces. Her bulky shoulders and chest are stopping her from bringing her elbows together, let alone the lower section of her arms.

"You must be going to the gym too much. What good is that doing you?"

Sylvia shows Jade a variation, one that mimics the effects of Garudasana without requiring the same degree of mobility.

"I hope you won't be going to the gym with Jade, Rose. It won't be doing you any good."

After class, Sylvia comes around to my flat for dinner. I have a few other friends around, and Sylvia is delighted to attend. We open a bottle of wine.

Sylvia is the first friend I've made who is significantly older than me. Other septuagenarians I've interacted with have a dullness to them, like they've been in a deep slumber before I started talking to them.

"So, Rose, is it serious with Jade?" Sylvia asks when Jade is out of the room.

"Not sure. I think it's too early to tell." I turn the question back on her. "What about with Terry? Is that serious?"

"Oh, who knows, Rose. When you get to my age, you'll see that life is never what you expect." She brings her wine glass to her lips.

My question about her relationship is mostly in jest. I know that she and Terry have been together for over fifteen years. To me they seem settled and stable. I didn't know people could still be bothered with the rigamarole of dating at her age.

"Who knows how things with Terry will turn out. Maybe my next one will be a woman."

*

People who study engineering take pride in the fact that it's a very practical, industry-focussed field—a fact that they sometimes hold over people who have chosen other life paths. Engineers literally create the pillars of society, they argue. Strong, structurally sound pillars.

I studied mechatronics engineering. "Mechatronics" is a portmanteau of "mechanical" and "electronic". It concerns machines with embedded software that are capable of autonomous movements. From the outside it sounds glamorous, like we're creating the next generation of robots with advanced AI systems. In reality, we design washing machines and elevators.

When I started studying, I found that engineering presented a way of thinking that justified abstraction and placed systematic thinking on a pedestal. In many of my male friends I observed a manufactured divide between "rational" and "emotional" thought, and a hierarchy based on their suitability for decision-making. My friends went through break-ups where they seemed to have no awareness of how their lack of communication had affected the relationship, but they still prided themselves on their inability to express their feelings. It's as if they were immune to their emotions, rather than just ignorant of them.

During this time I was living with my friend Rosa, a PhD physics student. In our flat we commiserated with each other over our shared experiences with engineers and physicists, how they seem to live under a self-inflicted veil. She described a realisation she'd had during a conference talk about the mind–body relationship—that most physicists thought of their bodies as glorified containers for their brains, which was the only part they cared about. Their bodies were fleshy transport systems, happy to eat the same bulk-made meal, needing physical movement only for maintenance purposes.

I'd thought I was above this type of over-intellectualising, but in my yoga practice I was finding that good teachers often reprimanded me for thinking too much. There was an aspect of the poses, or asana, that I treated like a puzzle, as if I could achieve the perfect posture by mechanically pushing and pulling the right parts of my body until everything fell into place. This was about control rather than awareness, and once I learned to mentally step back and observe, I started learning how to engage with my body. What I'd started developing was my proprioceptive sense—a person's sense of where their body is in space without having to look.

I researched how it worked on an anatomical level: the body's skeletal muscles contain sensory fibres, each wrapped by sensory nerves that detect changes in the muscle's length. From this, the brain knows which muscles are contracting and can build an internal map of the body, complete with the position of joints and appendages. While the theory was interesting, proprioception wasn't something I could develop just by understanding the concept. That would only come with practice.

*

At Sylvia's persuasion, I attend my first yoga retreat with her in the Coromandel. We drive up the entranceway of the retreat centre, flanked by pink Himalayan salt crystals and bronze Buddha statues. A team of beaming white people greet us, clad in naturally dyed fibres. The older woman in the centre steps forward and introduces herself as the manager. Her name is Shanti. Shanti focusses her intention deeply on me as she asks for my name. She holds my gaze and slowly repeats my name back to me, still beaming. After she performs this ritual on Sylvia, we are introduced to the other staff, all wwoofers. One of them has dreads. Sylvia and I leave the welcoming circle and unroll our mats in the octagonal yoga room.

Silence falls as the teacher ambles into the octagon. He's in his late fifties, with dark hair streaking to silver at the temples. He asks those with injuries to identify themselves. There's one woman whose left shoulder is prone to dislocation, and another who lost her left kneecap in a car accident. Before I am confident with everyone's names, I identify them by their injuries.

For two of these women, Iyengar yoga was instrumental in their recovery. I get to know them over the course of the retreat. One of the women carries around a book about nurturing the "divine feminine" and talks to me about how life-changing it was for her to have found yoga. I can draw many parallels between our experiences with yoga, but something holds me back from the clear-eyed devotion that she shows. I wonder if I

72

would feel differently if yoga had helped me through an injury like hers. Would I be more evangelical about its holistic benefits?

From a young age, I've had a mental block with the idea of a higher power. When my parents first moved to New Zealand, upon the recommendation of a friend they joined a church to learn English. Churches are abundant in dual Chinese–English resource material. I was taken along to home groups and Sunday school, where I learned tenets of faith, like loving God above all. I was a seven-year-old who had just learned about God but had loved my parents my entire life. It worried me, this eternal damnation I would suffer if I didn't correct the hierarchy of my affections. When we left the church less than a year later, these thoughts slipped out of my mind.

Later we moved to Auckland and my parents decided to join a Taiwanese Buddhist church so they could have a Chinese community. Us kids were left to run around while the adults listened to the sermon, but when it came time for the kowtows we were shepherded into the hall, where we kneeled on thin cushions to press our foreheads into the floor. Despite the several hundred-odd kowtows to endure, it was something I looked forward to every week. But one day, without warning, we stopped going. I never got a chance to say goodbye to my friends.

Years later I found out that my parents had been invited to attend a formal induction ceremony into the church. They turned up, perhaps expecting to perform more kowtows than usual. Instead, a woman in the congregation was possessed by the spirit of a male deity. She swaggered around the hall, intoning scripture in the drawl typified by that period of history. Her posture, her walk, her speech patterns had all changed in a snap. After witnessing this, my parents never took us back.

In my parents' fifteen years at the dairy, the shop has closed only once. My mum went to hospital for a hysterectomy, and my dad traded his plastic seat behind the takeaway counter for a plastic chair in the hospital waiting room. I came back to Whanganui from Wellington. My mum had three nights to spend in recovery, and the shop was closed for only the day of her procedure; over the following days a second pair of hands was needed for the morning, lunch and dinner rushes. In those evenings we would visit with a big thermos of 粥, and I would eat the ice cream from her abandoned dinner.

Everything had gone smoothly. The odds of complications had always been low, but we all carried our own anxieties regardless. The medical report that my mum had been given was written in clipped technical language, and I fretted that something bad would come from the communication barrier between the hospital staff and her. I happened to be in the room when a physician doing the rounds came by post-op, and when I went to translate I found she didn't need me to.

Unlike my grandmother's puckered belly, three small scars are the only signs of the procedure on my mother's body. By the end of the week she was back in the dairy, doing all her regular tasks except the ones that required her to lift her hands above her head. I wonder how she felt, whether the general anaesthetic still dragged in her system, or whether she was just relieved to be without her uterus. It had needed to be removed because she had developed fibroids, clumpy growths that leeched blood out of her body. She had not given enough attention to this extra menstrual flow until a routine blood test showed dangerously low levels of iron. I wonder how she'd had the energy to work every day before this was discovered. Perhaps her body had an immense capacity for endurance; perhaps she was simply too busy to notice.

*

In a full hip replacement operation, an incision is made across the back of the hip. Muscles are detached from the pelvis and the femur. The damaged femur ball is sawn off, and a metal ball with a stem extending into the cavity of the bone is fitted in its place. Crumbly cartilage is shaved from the hip socket, and a plastic socket is attached with bone cement.

It takes time for the muscles to firm up again and lock the joint in place. Dislocation is uncommon, but there is a higher risk of it in the first few months of recovery.

"Before yoga, I couldn't walk!" Sylvia tells me over dinner. "My hips were so tight! Oh, it was horrible, Rose, you wouldn't have believed how bad it was!"

It's true; I can't imagine an immobile version of Sylvia. I've just seen her do the full splits, followed by a five-minute headstand. Her joints swivel smoothly through their full range of motion. She reaches for the bean salad and starts to describe at length *just* how bad it was. "I couldn't walk more than five steps! I had to give up my golf! I delayed the operation for as long as I could, I wanted to see how far I could get with my yoga."

At the age of fifty, Sylvia couldn't walk more than a hundred metres unaided and doctors told her she needed two full replacements of her arthritic hips. This is why she started doing yoga in the first place—to delay the intensive surgery as long as possible.

"And as soon as I was awake after the surgery, I was doing as much yoga as I could!"

"Is that a good idea so soon after a major surgery?" I ask.

"Well—"

Terry cuts in. "It was against the doctor's orders."

"Oh, rubbish! Those doctors don't know tosh, the worst

thing you can do for the body is to stay in bed and let it stiffen up!"

Terry and I glance at each other. He rolls his eyes at me. "Yes, dear, you know more than all the medical professionals."

Our friendship is unusual in so many ways. At my age she would have been living in England, newly married and spending her days hitting balls on the tennis court. She worked as a florist, a gym owner and a mum before deciding in her fifties to follow her daughter Fiona to New Zealand. Her husband came out with her, but he couldn't cope with the change to their settled lives. So she left him and he returned alone to England.

I used to fear growing older. I saw it as a slow act of narrowing, where the body and mind stiffen and restrict. But that isn't true for Sylvia. She has held on to her ability to adapt.

When my dad turns fifty, he purchases a treadmill. Every evening after work, he runs for half an hour. He asks if I can buy him a step counter. I do some research online and settle on a mid-range Fitbit, one that measures heart rate but doesn't send emails. I buy myself one at the same time, and we become friends on the Fitbit app.

My dad almost always wins the step count. Between his daily run and pacing the length of the dairy, he averages 18,000 steps a day. Even if he forgets to wear the device during the work day, his half-hour run allows him to hit the 10,000 steps recommended by the app.

Around the same time, my brother starts rowing at high school. Before rowing, he was a bit pudgy, like the rest of the family. Now he gets up at 5am five days a week and bikes across town to rowing training. "你的弟弟划船划得好辛苦，我们给他做饭补营养也好辛苦啊。" | "Your brother works so hard

76

at rowing, we work so hard keeping him fed," my mum tells me over the phone.

When I go home that Christmas, I get a shock. My dad has lost about twenty kilograms, and it looks like my brother has put on the same amount in muscle mass. Dad is the skinniest I've ever seen him, the skinniest he's been since high school. Matthew is the widest I've ever seen him. He's got the Lù family thighs now. Even at rest, the muscles that make up his quadriceps are clearly defined and bulging.

I've brought my yoga mat with me. My mum sees me practising in the lounge. "哎呀！我们家的人都变成运动员了！就剩下了我懒着不锻炼！" | "Aiya! Our family members have all become sport stars! Just lazy me left!"

At New Year, my mum, my brother and I take a road trip around the North Island. It's my dad's turn to mind the shop this holiday season. We spend a couple of days in the Hawke's Bay, and my mum and brother come to a yoga class with me.

I catch up with Sylvia over coffee afterwards. Before she even opens her mouth, I know what she'll say about my brother. "He needs to stop rowing. All that's doing is restricting his movement. Gosh, his hamstrings are tight!"

She adds more water to her coffee. Her usual order is a flat white, and an entire pot of hot water to dilute it.

"Your mother has promise, but she spent the entire time trying to help your brother. If she focussed on herself, she'd have a good practice."

# ALL WHO LIVE ON ISLANDS

Do you remember the food at school camps? The plastic cereal dispensers spitting out cornflakes and Ricies for us kids, and Sultana Bran for the teachers. Fruit salad from a one-kilogram can, pieces of apple and pear steeped in syrup for so long that they all tasted the same. And for dinner, lasagne, in industrial-sized baking trays.

Lasagne was a dish I'd only heard about, and I couldn't wait to try it. I knew it had mince, tomatoes and cheese, and that the construction involved layering. I learned the word lasagne long before I had my first bite. I had seen the word written down, I had heard it spoken aloud, and my brain had put two and two together. Who would have guessed that the *g* and the *n* next to each other would have produced that sound?

A red slab was slopped onto my plate. I fumbled with the knife and fork. The lasagne tasted unlike any food I ate at home. Further down the table I could see Winnie pushing her food around her plate. My cheeks reddened. I averted my gaze.

I hoped I didn't look as unpractised with the knife and fork as she did.

Winnie was my buddy at school camp and I wasn't happy about it. Winnie didn't get jokes. Winnie wore tracksuits with embroidered teddy bears and didn't know she was supposed to be embarrassed. When Winnie started at school, teachers made sure to introduce us, even though we weren't in the same class.

I grew up being told that I was Chinese. The declaration came whenever I barricaded myself in my room and refused to go to Saturday morning Mandarin classes. My mum yelled at me, "你是中国人! 必须学汉语!" | "You are Chinese! You must learn Mandarin!" It came when I was running through the playground, kicking up bark with my feet. "Hey, ching chong!" yelled some older boys, holding court in the highest point of the wooden structure. It came from the teachers who paired me up with Winnie at school camp. I knew what people chose to see first about me, and it wasn't how I wanted to be perceived.

There was no real understanding in the way my non-Asian peers and teachers applied the label "Chinese". Their notion of "Chinese" was a wisp, made of snatches of caricature and ignorance. As I child I often felt angry about being seen in this way, but there was nothing I could do about it. I was too young to know how to articulate these feelings, and even if I did, no one around me would have understood.

This was Palmerston North in 1999. We didn't have much of a Chinese community. My parents didn't allow me to go to the homes of my Pākehā school friends, which felt extremely unfair. Later I realised how hard it must have been for them to navigate the rituals of play dates in a foreign culture.

To pass the time, I turned to books. There must have been a period in which I wasn't confident with English, but I quickly became the top reader in the class. My only memory from ESOL is of making an egg-carton pastiche of the Very Hungry Caterpillar, bored by the picture book as it was below my reading level. I checked out the maximum number of books allowed from the library. I read in the car. I read on the toilet. I read in the shower. I read when I should have been sleeping. I read so much that my mum started to worry about my constant yawning at the breakfast table and imposed a five-book limit on my weekly library trips. Reading was how I learned about British and American children my age. Their lives were filled with sleepless sleepovers, bright piñatas at birthday parties, the punishment of "grounding". There were stories about New Zealand children too: I read about Alex Archer, reaching arm over arm to defeat her rival and earn a place at the Commonwealth Games.

In our first eight years in New Zealand, my family moved through four cities and eight houses. Every time I changed schools, I had to start over again. I needed to reestablish my presentation to others, to be seen as something different to whatever stereotypes of "Asian" they held. I was scarcely ten years old and these strategies of adaptation were critical to my survival in the cultural milieux around me. My primary school in suburban Palmerston North operated completely differently from the one in Panmure, South Auckland, and then again from the melting pot of Mt Roskill Intermediate.

Amidst all this change, the universe of books was reassuringly stable. I could disappear into *Animorphs* and be back with Jake and the gang, wondering what Cinnabon tasted like. Books, along with TV, gave me a lens into the cultural norms of the Pākehā majority. It was a refracted lens, given that the books I was reading and TV shows I was watching were predominantly British and American. But the cultures were close enough for me to learn how to behave like the other kids, how to downplay the parts of my life that needed explanation.

In my first year of high school we moved again, this time to Whanganui. I sobbed for the entire car ride. I didn't want to leave Auckland. Whanganui was a hard place to adjust to, especially coming from Mt Roskill, where I had a group of Chinese and Indian friends. I was noticeably different once again. There were fewer than five Asian kids in my year group, and most of the student body couldn't conceive of life outside of Whanganui. Someone started a joke that my family ate cats. It was like the joke had nine lives; when I thought it was dead and gone it always came back. School was a place ruled by arrogance and machismo, and the teachers excused bad behaviour with "boys will be boys". Compared with some of the stories told about other kids, I counted myself lucky.

The collection at the Whanganui library was far smaller than I was used to in Auckland, but I made do. I read books about being in love and having sex for the first time, and learned that the world didn't end when a relationship was over. I read about overcoming eating disorders and how you should accept yourself the way you are. I read books that depicted subjects like grief, mental illnesses and parental separation with compassion and sensitivity—but I never encountered a character who was going through the process of enforced adaptation, of learning to navigate a liminal space where you're not quite one thing or the other.

Of all the books I read during my school years, I can recall only a handful of characters of East Asian ethnicity. There was ditzy artist Claudia Kishi from *The Baby-Sitter's Club*, whose room in her Japanese–American household was chosen as the club's meeting place because she had the best snacks and a private phoneline. Then Cho Chang from *Harry Potter*, with her ethnically ambiguous name—mixing "Cho", a common Korean surname, with "Chang", a common Chinese surname. Then came *Chinese Cinderella* by Adeline Yen Mah, a memoir about an unlucky and unloved Chinese daughter—the only English-language novel of its kind I had access to.

Bereft of more complex views about China, I slowly started believing the same stereotypes as the people around me. People who looked like me were relegated to supporting roles, never the leading ones. We could talk about where we came from, but only in a way that further entrenched ideas of the brutality of non-white cultures. I thought of China as an impoverished, totalitarian and lacklustre country, and books, TV and movies never showed me anything to the contrary. Besides, why else would we have left? Why else would my parents have renounced the place?

It provokes strange reactions in us, to be almost invisible in the stories we read. Graci Kim, an Auckland-raised writer, talks about her experience completing a writing assignment about her family at primary school. Her teacher pulled her aside because Graci had described herself and her parents as being "blond, with blue eyes", despite their black hair and brown eyes. As a child, she had thought that this physical description was a grammatical rule or convention, like capitalising proper nouns. She had thought that in books it was incorrect to write characters who looked like us.

\*

I left Whanganui to go to university in Christchurch. By this time I had become an expert at presenting myself as a certain type of Chinese. I made sure people could see me by my New

Zealand accent, and any other interpretation was a fault of theirs. I understood where I was from as a binary, with New Zealand on one side and China on the other. I could hear racism in the disbelief that I was "from" Whanganui, and in the amazement that my English was so good. However, I never saw a problem with labelling myself a "banana", or when Pākehā friends commented that they "forgot" I had a race.

For me, Chinese culture was defined by an absence, a set of negative qualities that I was determined not to uphold. Given my new independent life at university, I had more urgent experiences to seek than those of a culture I'd spent my life keeping at bay. I spent my time studying in the engineering computer lab, hanging out with my flatmates, or dancing to bands at Goodbye Blue Monday before the 2011 earthquake closed the CBD. I never got too complacent, as the city would inevitably serve me reminders that I was not welcome. Everyday racism had gall in Christchurch. But my day-to-day existence was insulated by the whiteness of the communities I inhabited, providing a thick layer of fat for me to hide behind. At the time, what bothered me was the lack of gender diversity in the engineering department and the Christchurch music scene.

It wasn't until I moved to Wellington after university that I started to realise that something about how I saw race was off. I was volunteering as a phone counsellor at Youthline, and in one training session I heard that another trainee, Sophie, had gone to school in Hong Kong. I blithely commented to her, "Oh, but your English is so good!" Our supervisor, also of Chinese heritage, overheard and cracked up at my faux pas. Sophie had received her schooling entirely in English, from an international school. In my mind I had drawn a line in the sand—me and everyone who had arrived in New Zealand before me were on one side; international students and later immigrants were on the other. Due to this categorisation, I had unconsciously made a series of incorrect assumptions about Sophie. I had acquired a passive form of racism that is pervasive among well-intentioned New Zealanders, one born of unaddressed ignorance. I had leaned into the idea that there were right and wrong types of immigrants, and in my desperation to be seen as one of the good ones, the ones who assimilated and spoke perfect English, it was necessary to cast out others who did not do the same.

Around this time I reconnected with an old friend, Lucy, from my intermediate school in Auckland. She invited me to a hot pot gathering at her house, a plaster orange monstrosity in a convenient location. I turned up with a packet of fish tofu and was surprised that everyone looked and talked like me. The majority of them were Aucklanders who had moved to Wellington for work. For them, it was the first time being in an environment where the ratio of Asian to Pākehā people wasn't one to one.

Lucy and her friends reminisced about spending semesters abroad in China and regular visits with family. I was enthralled when they spoke of the ease with which their Chinese identity ebbed and flowed in their lives. For me, China had frozen when we left. December 1995 had become a still frame, the snapshot pinning my family's image of China. We had left while China was on the cusp of an exponential boom, as if the whole country was taking a preparatory breath. I had no memory of what the Pǔdōng skyline looked like. I was five years old and everything about that time was tawny and subdued.

Since leaving, I'd only been back to China twice: a barely remembered trip at eight years old, and another, begrudgingly, at twenty-one. As there weren't many other points of reference, I had assumed that it was normal not to have any contact with family back in China. But now, hearing my new friends discuss their experiences with modern China, understanding all the different paths their families took to emigrate, it framed my life in a different light. It piqued my curiosity about this place that I was always told I was from, but knew next to nothing about. I habitually pushed back against being Chinese, but I realised what I was railing against was a spectre, one concocted from a lifetime of misinformation.

*

In 2016, I decided to embark on the rite of passage for privileged New Zealanders: a big OE. My itinerary traced an arc through South and East Asia, with the bulk of my time spent in China. My first stop there was Chéngdū, the provincial capital of Sìchuān. Despite it being the fifth most populous city in China, with an urban population of over ten million, the majority of my Pākehā friends had never heard its name.

My first few weeks in Chéngdū were difficult. The cultural difference punched like raw ginger—the incessant honking of vehicles, the sharp shouts, the freedom of people's behaviour in public, street corners crowded with 串串 | chuànchuàn carts operating well past midnight. I was surprised by how modern and convenient the cities were. I couldn't understand the local Sìchuān dialect, and residents were loath to switch to Mandarin when they spoke to me.

I discovered that learning a language was less about memorising words and more about using them in different ways. "你吃了吗?" | "Have you eaten?" is a way to say "How are you?" In shops, staff enquired with "请问你需要些什么?" | "What do you need?" rather than "May I help you?"—changing the subject of the sentence to suit a less self-centred culture.

I started to realise that all the times my parents and I had talked past each other were likely a result of cultural and generational misunderstandings rather than a lack of a common language.

I took every opportunity to talk to people about their lives. The slowness of my Mandarin speech meant I did more listening than talking. Listening to these stories undid the assumptions I held about China, and I could hear people's joy and pride about being from here. Details of everyday habits and rituals illuminated a depth and complexity that I hadn't considered before. I heard stories seldom told in Western media, and stories I'd heard often but this time from a sinocentric point of view. I was fascinated by the ways in which people made sense of their place in the world, and the chorus of their opinions across this big land. Coming from Aotearoa, a country of people humble to a fault, I never expected Chinese people to be so damn proud. People had extensive knowledge of Chinese history, classical literature, the preparation of specialty foods in different regions.

In my conversations, the topic of home often came up. There were two reasons: the high volume of internal migration in China, and my accent. Native 普通话 | standard Mandarin speakers correctly ascertained that I didn't grow up in China. From my use of 好 rather than 很 as an intensifier many guessed I was Taiwanese, followed by Hong Kongese, Malaysian or Singaporean. New Zealand always came as a surprise to them.

I would then qualify that 我的老家是上海 | my hometown is Shànghǎi. Neither part of my answer was ever challenged. In one of these first exchanges, I was given the word 华裔, a term for overseas Chinese people. In China, I wore a term like "expatriate". Unlike the other word, 外国人 | foreigners. Unlike the labels I was given back home.

86

The stories I heard began to fill the twenty-year gap of my family's absence, and painted a picture of the things that we had left behind. I saw the shape of the life that nearly could have been mine, and saw the differences as texture and colour: neither good nor bad; they simply were. There was such breadth in what it meant to be Chinese, so much that was invisible within the monoscopic view presented in New Zealand.

I observed how the staple foods changed with geography and climate, switching from rice to wheat or potato. My ear learned to associate accents with regions: the rolling Sìchuān speech, the 儿 sprinkled at the end of Běijīngers' sentences. China's land area is roughly the same as Europe, and each province has a culture and language as distinct as those of the individual countries of Europe.

I learned of the rampant inequalities created by the 户籍制度 | household registration system; my 姑妈 | aunt casually mentioned over dinner that she could never retire, because her rural designation meant she didn't have access to the pension. In one hostel I was surprised to meet a Middle Eastern–looking man who spoke perfect Mandarin. He was from Xīnjiāng, and three hours after his arrival a pair of police officers showed up to double-check all of his documents. The standard check-in process for accommodation involved official identification being taken and scanned, and this administrative procedure took on a new weight.

All of this abolished the stereotypes that I held about any singular Chinese identity, despite what official party lines in China, and New Zealand's lack of interest in non-English speaking cultures, had led me to believe. I accepted being Chinese only when I had learned enough about China to see that any blanket statement about a country of 1.4 billion people was meaningless. I became more assured about being from

Aotearoa *and* being from China—something I repeatedly had to explain to my Pākehā friends, who saw my cultural identity as a needle wavering between the two places. At one point I had seen it that way too, but now I view it as a symbiotic relationship, two twinned vines growing in tandem.

Before I spent this time in China, I had never missed it. I hadn't known what to miss. I focussed only on its deficits—on the perceived wrongness of somewhere that is different. I was prepared to be frustrated by the Great Firewall, to encounter the brutality of people being left behind by rapid economic change, but once I came back to New Zealand I yearned for the small moments that had defined my experience of China: riding bicycles on chaotic roads but never feeling unsafe, the flamboyant mannerisms of retirees playing cards in public parks, how the smells of different lives all spilled onto the street.

*

After my trip, I wanted to engage more in the Chinese community in Aotearoa New Zealand. Emma Ng's book *Old Asian, New Asian*, a pithy account of Asian New Zealand history, had just been published. The book started as an essay on the website *The Pantograph Punch* in response to shoddy statistical "analysis" by Phil Twyford of the Labour Party. He drew a dubious causation between "Asian-sounding last names", the aforementioned Asians' residency status, and the Auckland housing crisis. Ng rightly pointed out that this scapegoating was just the latest in a litany of racist acts towards Asian New Zealanders. Its roots run deep: for as long as Pākehā have colonised Aotearoa, they have restricted the entry of non-white people.

*Old Asian, New Asian* helped me situate my experience in the greater arc of the Asian New Zealand experience. It reminded me that racism is often introduced and sanctioned by the state. Public backlash towards Chinese gold miners resulted in the Chinese Immigrants Act of 1881. This act introduced a "poll tax"—a tax of £10, increasing to £100 in 1896—on the head of each Chinese man who sailed steerage with the livestock to New Zealand. As the writer and musician Kristen Ng has observed, "And so marked the beginning of a long Kiwi tradition—blaming immigrants for failures in the New Zealand economy." The policy wasn't abolished until 1944. The Chinese community had to wait longer still, until 2002, for a formal apology from Helen Clark, New Zealand's prime minister at the time.

It was another policy change that permitted my family's entry to New Zealand. We came after modifications to immigration laws in 1987 and 1991, which saw the removal of a "preferred race" clause and the introduction of a points-based system that my young, university-educated and relatively wealthy parents met. Like many migrants, they were fleeced by an immigration broker, who had them pay the 2019 equivalent of $10,000 for helping them to navigate the administrative system of a foreign country. This broker's fee was still about a quarter of what my family would have paid under the poll tax, and, for the trouble, at least we received a shuttle from the airport and accommodation in Auckland for the first few weeks.

We arrived in January 1996, when Aotearoa was in the middle of a steady decade of immigration from Asia. People came from China, Japan, Korea, India, the Philippines and Sri Lanka, and this prompted a new wave of anti-Asian sentiment. In that same year Winston Peters campaigned against immigration, citing "the Asian Invasion". It was an unsettling time both for us newcomers and established Asian communities, many of whom were third-generation descendants of Poll Tax migrants.

Before this there had been a few decades of relative peace, but now the timbre of everyday interactions was changing. Racism drew broad, rough strokes, erasing and reducing people; Asian New Zealanders became a maligned Other.

This came out of the blue for many Asian New Zealanders, such as the parents of Tze Ming Mok, an essayist and sociopolitical commentator. Her Singaporean mother and Malaysian father came here in 1973 as part of an initiative by the New Zealand government to recruit Commonwealth Asian doctors. Her parents were native English speakers and received a fairly warm welcome from the hospital system. Back then, there were so few doctors that patients knew they were lucky to take what they could get.

After almost two decades of living in New Zealand, the family was not prepared for the crescendo of racism in the 1990s. Though they were somewhat insulated by their establishment in respected professions, the increase of direct racism in their lives was hard to take. Migrants and tangata whenua are underrepresented in positions of power in Aotearoa, and inherent in our lives is a sense of precarity. The way we are treated can change at any time, due to forces outside our control.

In my reading I began to look for personal stories. I found Helene Wong's memoir *Being Chinese*, which follows her childhood in a fruit shop in 1940s Utiku and her coming of age under Muldoon's aggressive economic policies as she chased an understanding of her Chinese identity.

Wong describes a trip back to her parents' birthplace, Shātóu, a village in the Zēngchéng district of Guǎngzhōu. She found her ancestral home rural and undeveloped, with unpaved roads that squished beneath her cousin's bare feet.

She depended on her parents to help her communicate, and while she found nonverbal ways to connect with other family members, a lot was left unsaid.

It was a cathartic and important experience for her, but it felt at odds with my time in China. The Shànghǎi I'd gone back to was a global city, and my Mandarin meant I could travel independently. Although migrants tend to be swept under one label, each generation, not to mention each person, has a specific and contradictory encounter with migration.

I turned to books written by my generation of migrants, and the majority I found were of Australian or American ilk. New Zealand has similar historical touchstones to these other British colonies; Chinese gold miners in the United States and Australia were also affected by race-based policies, like the Chinese Exclusion Act of 1883 and the White Australia policy, formally established in 1901. These stories were written by people barely a decade older than me, and we had come of age in similarly uneasy times. We sat and watched in our colonised homes as the white majority grappled with changing ethnic demographics and indigenous sovereignty.

Stories from the modern diaspora come with their own tropes: the childhood wish for blond hair, being teased by white kids over your smelly lunch, the same white kids growing up to be white adults critiquing the authenticity of your cuisine. Some of these tropes I identified with; others I did not.

I discovered that the majority of Chinese families showed love through food rather than physical or verbal affection, unlike my family who would hug me when I came home *and* prepare my favourite dishes. When I asked my parents about the Cultural Revolution, knowing that my dad's side of the family was educated, their response was nonchalant. For them, the biggest disruption was that school stopped for a while.

Any of my theories on why are speculative; perhaps the administration of their small village wasn't worth crossing the Yangtze River for. Stories resonated for me when they illuminated the parts of my family and upbringing that felt unique to us.

It was this specificity that I sought. Discrimination was a universal theme in diasporic Asian literature, but reading about it was not a novel experience. I wanted literature to show me things that I couldn't already identify. The revelations I sought were the quiet kind, like the fact that the 馄饨 in Shànghǎi are characteristically small, or the feeling of contentment when you hear a conversation in your mother tongue. For these insights the mirror needed to be held closer, so that it could take in the small details of my experience. This is where literature from elsewhere fell short. Aotearoa has a particular isolation that cannot be found anywhere else—an isolation of pointed significance to migrants. I grew up in a town of forty thousand people rather than a city the size of San Francisco or Melbourne. Here there is no Chinatown to gentrify, no fraternities at college. I wanted stories that reflected the particularities of the migrant experience in Aotearoa.

*

In March 2018 I arrived at Bill Manhire House like many other students, flustered from the near-vertical climb to the university. I was intimidated by my classmates, many of whom had been published extensively. On the walls there were austere black-and-white photographs of past Writers in Residence, who gazed down with the full knowledge that I was an illiterate STEM major clown who hadn't read any of their works.

My classmates suffered from impostor syndrome too, but this knowledge did not abate my anxiety. Some of them had coveted a spot in this creative writing programme since high school, and had only gained entry on a second or third application. I had only heard of the International Institute of Modern Letters a few years ago when some of my friends went through the programme. Before moving to Wellington no one around me valued literature enough to know about a programme like this, let alone pursue it.

At the end of high school I had talked to my parents about studying English at university. They responded by laughing. "学了英文想干嘛?" | "What are you going to do with an English degree?" they said. "当老师吗? 你其实有其他更好的选择。" | "Become a teacher? You can do better than that." The careers counsellor at my school wasn't much better. While he didn't mock me, he didn't understand that I needed practical advice to persuade my parents—and perhaps even myself—that a degree in English would be a good choice for my future.

An early assignment at the IIML was to attend five sessions at Wellington Readers and Writers week. At one event I sat next to Sharon Lam and Maria Samuela, who had both finished degrees in creative writing the previous year. Sharon and I connected over our mutual experience of being the only Asian person in our years. We joked about establishing an "Asians of the IIML" club. In the school's entire lauded history, there has been only a handful of Asian graduates. I suspect it's much the same in other creative writing schools around the country.

It's not impossible to establish yourself as a writer in New Zealand without doing a master's programme, but it can't be easy either. It's a rare opportunity to focus and develop your writing under the guidance of established writers, and to be handed the social connections that creative writing schools accumulate. For me, an untrained and unnetworked outsider, it seemed a direct route into the world of literature and publishing.

Wellington was home to a number of writers who were significant to me, including the poets Nina Powles, Chris Tse and Gregory Kan. At the IIML, all three wrote what would become their first collections of poetry: Powles's was a collection that focussed on five women in Aotearoa's history, Tse's centered on the murder of Joe Kum Yung on Haining Street, and Kan's was a woven exploration of his family history and that of poet Robin Hyde.

As I read their work I saw the topic of cultural identity drifting in and out of focus, like it did during my year at the creative writing school. At times it would come into sharp focus, but most of the time it floated around me like dust motes. For me, my creative writing degree was a culmination of an intense period of personal exploration and reconnection with Chinese culture. If I had done it at a different time in my life, I would have written something very different, something with less discussion of my cultural identity.

A charming yet claustrophobic feature of Wellington is the relative ease with which connections are made. During the year I found a greater community of Asian arts practitioners, primarily during the Asian Aotearoa Arts Huì organised by Kerry Ann Lee. Considering the cultural uniformity of my creative writing class, I needed to have people I could talk to without giving them lots of background information. My classmates didn't share the specific anxieties I had about my writing and how I would be read, so I felt fortunate to make friends like Sharon Lam, whose dry commentary helped me keep my perspective.

Each writer in my class went through their own journey with their work. They had their individual struggles. But, to quote writer Jenny Zhang, my Pākehā contemporaries were free to write without "the millstone of *but is this authentic /*

*representative / good for black / Asian / Latino / native people?* hanging from their necks".

This observation comes from an essay titled "They Pretend to Be Us While Pretending We Don't Exist". It was a formative text for me in my year at the IIML. The essay describes an act of deceit by an established white American poet who, after having a particular poem rejected forty times, decides to increase his luck by submitting it under a Chinese pen name.

"To be Other in America is to be coveted and hated at the same time," Zhang writes, speaking to the jealousy her white classmates at the Iowa Writers' Workshop expressed towards her. They assumed that she'd have an easy ride in the publishing industry due to her ethnicity, without acknowledging the negative aspects of being a racial minority in America.

Almost a decade separates my and Zhang's times in creative writing programmes, and there are a few notable differences in our classroom dynamics. Compared with Zhang's, my classmates were very close and invested in one another's work, and we were generous in celebrating one another's successes. This was the luck of the draw; some creative writing classes gel together better than others. I heard that when classmates are mutually supportive, everyone's writing gets stronger.

Social media has also become a greater influence in the time between my degree and Zhang's. People are more conscious of the impact of their words, at least in the liberal circles the readership of this book will likely travel in. Though no one was thoughtless enough to imply that being a minority was an advantage, some classmates looked to me as the arbiter of racial bias in their work, often on cultures I had no knowledge about. Writers of colour worry about being "authentic" and being good representatives for their own communities; Pākehā writers worry about looking racially conscious.

But when it comes to addressing underlying racial injustices, most Pākehā have no skin in the game. Why are so many Pākehā rushing to do an introductory course in te reo Māori so that they can correct their pronunciation, without sticking around for the intermediate and advanced classes? Why are we so quick to point to Australia when our own poor race relations are scrutinised? Why are companies photographing yellow and brown employees for their advertising campaigns while their executive boards are lily-white? Why am I being asked to give something a "sensitivity read", instead of Pākehā sharing or even giving up their positions of power in the Aotearoa publishing industry to people of colour?

*

In her lecture "Poutokomanawa", presented at the Auckland Writers Festival in 2017, Tina Makereti gave an ethnic breakdown of New Zealand publishing in 2015. In that year, just 2 per cent of books were written by Asian authors, 4 per cent by Pasifika peoples and 6 per cent by Māori. Compared with national demographics, all of these groups are severely underrepresented, and Asian people particularly so. What are the stories we are unable to hear?

Two kilometres away from my parents' dairy and takeaway shop, a Chinese couple from Fújiàn run a similar family business. The Fújiàn couple have a daughter too, a year older than me. After she completed her university degree, her parents asked her to come back to Whanganui to help them run the business. It's a decision that her parents regret, as it's made it harder for her to find the type of work that matches her qualifications. She graduated with an MBA earlier this year and is living with her parents while she looks for work, stuck in the twilight of being overqualified but under-experienced, with few 关系 | social connections to use as leverage.

At one point we lived only a few kilometres apart, but now it's hard for me to reconcile the distance between my life and hers. For her, pursuing a vocation that is creative rather than economically secure would be unfeasible. The stories that filter out of the Chinese community and into mainstream New Zealand are the ones of success and integration, and that these stories are so celebrated only reinforces the damaging stereotypes that all immigrants are well-behaved and hard-working. Left in silence are the immigrants who don't make it, who are exploited, who bow to the voices that shout at them, "Go home."

I wonder what happened to my friend Julia, who I walked home with every day for a year. She had a copy of the *Pokémon* handbook and we would spend hours poring over it at her house. Before intermediate started, her family moved back to China for work-related reasons, and I was too young to keep in touch. How does she remember her time in Aotearoa?

What would enable my friend Bórén to tell his story? I met him during his relationship with my high-school friend Jared. He studied literature at university in Zhèjiāng, the neighbouring province to my birthplace of Shànghǎi. In 2016 he came to New Zealand as an international student, studying nursing in Invercargill while his parents pulled double shifts driving trucks to support him. He spent his downtime reading the English classics that I had never bothered with. To explain the lack of women in his life, Bórén told his parents that he aspired to be a monk.

I have a window into this other world, one set in the same physical plane as Aotearoa. It is hidden in plain sight by eyes that refuse to look, refuse to see that they are also New Zealand stories. Being granted the platform of a published book is rare for anyone, let alone someone from an ethnic group that is still excluded from the mainstream New Zealand identity. I feel a sense of responsibility with my work, because I know it will be seen as an act of Asian New Zealand representation. Many non-Asian readers will see the need to engage with only one text like this, but within one volume there will never be enough words to express the intricacies of our lives. There are more stories than there are publishers, production studios and galleries willing to support their creation.

For me, writing is a complex manoeuvre. I need to keep one eye roving forward while the other roves backwards through the window. There will be no true progress until there is acceptance for everyone who has come to New Zealand, no matter their place of origin, no matter their length of tenure on this land. I wonder what life in Aotearoa will be like in 2038, when our population is projected to be a third Māori, Asian and Pasifika. I wonder what our publishing industry will look like then.

I was born on one island, and I've come to live on a different one. 崇明岛 | Chóngmíng Island is a hundredth of the size of the North Island, and is currently being redeveloped as "Shànghǎi's backyard", a country respite from the fast-paced city.

The first time I went back, I ran up a muddy path to my grandparents' house. The second time I went back, all the streets were sealed and my grandparents' house had been demolished to make way for a new hospital. The last time I went back, I heard that a subway line from the city was in progress.

Once, I asked my grandfather how many generations of our family had been on the island. He said he didn't know for sure, but he thought it was his grandfather's grandfather who sailed here from the south, in the sixteenth or seventeenth century.

I asked if he knew who was on the island before we arrived. He waved his hand.

"住在岛上的人都是移民过来的," came his answer.

All who live on islands have to migrate.

# ALPHABET GAME

*America*

Every Wednesday I have lunch with Maggie. We meet on the varnished wooden steps outside the university bookshop. Maggie is easy to spot. Her hair is bright blond, almost white. A colour common on children, but it doesn't usually stay so naturally bright into adulthood.

Before we became friends, I knew her only by the luminescence of her hair. For years we travelled in similar Wellington social circles, always a degree of separation from each other. It took a while for our friendliness to grow from saying hi at parties to hanging out one on one. It's only this year that we've started having lunch regularly. It's partly due to circumstance; we're both based at the university while most people we know work in the central city.

We greet each other with a hug. She speaks with a lilting American accent, a remnant of her time in Colorado. There's a thrill in getting to know someone and discovering the different contours of each other's preferences. Maggie and I have covered a fair bit of ground in our weekly lunches. A recount of Wellington romantic history shows common links; a person I sort-of dated is her boyfriend of several years. We're both bisexual, but end up wasting more time on men. We play the counsellor role with friends who tend to circle listlessly around the same negative patterns of thought.

Our pasts are populated by people who have demanded our attention. This attraction to emotional intensity is a shared trait of ours. We're suckers for relationships with turbulent highs and lows that push against the limits of our emotional capacity.

But in our late twenties and early thirties, that type of interaction is tiring. It's impossible to sustain now that we have careers instead of part-time jobs, where enough sleep is vital. We articulate our emotional worlds to each other, but there's a different quality to it. There's no expectation beyond support. We speak of our feelings, but we don't draw the other into a contract. Our feelings are our own to hold.

*Berlin*

I video-call Viv. She's in Berlin, ten hours behind New Zealand. It's her Saturday morning and she natters to me about her work situation as she makes coffee. "I'm washing dishes at this café on Friday, Saturday and Sunday evenings. It keeps the weekdays free, and besides, I don't have a lot of friends here."

Viv was my best friend in Wellington before she moved, although at twenty-eight we're too old to use words like "best friend". When I was younger, my mum told me that I couldn't rely on friends as much as I could rely on family. Only family would look after you if you got sick; only family would love you enough to tell you your faults.

I think this sentiment reflects the difference between my life and my parents'. Before the move, my parents knew no one in New Zealand. Of course they made friends here, but the life of a new immigrant is unstable. Everyone kept moving away, looking for a patch of employment and opportunity to root down in. There was no guarantee that people would stick around to help.

Growing up here gave me a wider circle of friends. Given the cultural and generational differences, my parents couldn't help me with questions about love, study or work. They had never lived communally with people their own age, so they weren't familiar with that type of closeness. When Viv got sick, she would text me and I would cycle to her flat and cook her stewed apple.

*Carlton Ave*
My parents bought the dairy on Carlton Ave when I was thirteen. Halfway through my third-form year, I was plucked away from my friend group in Mt Roskill and had to start over in Whanganui. I didn't have much luck. Thankfully, it wasn't long before Text 2000 and MSN Messenger came along. I lived a double life, fingers and thumbs connecting me to friends I'd left in Auckland.

Kimberley and I became best friends through texting. We weren't close when I left Auckland—we were in the same class but didn't hang out at lunchtimes. Our long-distance friendship grew as we commiserated with each other about our strict parents and shared a love of pop-punk and emo bands. Her favourite band was Green Day and mine was Blink-182. It was an age of boredom and endless availability. We were content to text each other about nothing much, just so we had something to do.

When we ran out of stuff to talk about we'd play games, like the alphabet game. Someone came up with a category and we took turns to alphabetically name items in that category. Fruit, for example. I'd text "apple". She'd reply with "banana". I'd think for a bit, then send "cherry".

The letters in the latter half of the alphabet were hard. We allowed creative interpretations, like "vine grapes", or agreed to skip letters. Every night we fell asleep like this, mulling over an instrument that started with "q", or an animal that started with "v".

## Davies Bay

After Kimberley and I fell out in seventh form, we didn't speak for a number of years. Instead of talking to her, I compulsively talked about her to other people. I couldn't avoid the topic. I needed to make sense of that time. A frequent listener was my flatmate Jared, a friend from high school. His initial reaction was surprise. I hadn't behaved much differently at school during that time; there was no indication that something serious had happened in my life.

From time to time a mutual friend would give me a brief update about Kimberley's life. She was studying media and English at the University of Auckland. The banal tidbits about her life confused me even more. Had she changed overnight from the person I knew?

Occasionally we attended the same social gatherings, and felt obliged to keep things amicable for the benefit of our friends. After a few interactions like this, we started texting again. It was easy to pick up something so familiar, so habitual. At times it felt like nothing had changed, but there was something inert about our resumed relationship. We stuck to safe topics. I replied to her messages when I could, but not as a priority. She was still the person who knew the most about me, but I didn't go to her for advice. I couldn't. I was afraid of relapsing into that reliance, of crossing the delicate barrier that we'd established.

Kimberly started dating a boy called Reese. Since Aidan, this was the first boy she'd been serious about. The next time I was in Auckland we drove to his house out west in Titirangi. It was within walking distance of Davies Bay, where Reese swam most days. He led us out of his street and down a scramble of boulders to the shore. I hopped from rock to rock, eager to be in the water. Wriggling my toes in the sand, I turned to look for the others. Reese and Kimberly were still making their way. Reese gazed at her protectively, waiting for her. Her steps were small and cautious, one hand holding the rock face and the other holding Reese's.

*Epsom*

When I was eleven I started attending Mandarin lessons. The weekend classes were held at a primary school in Epsom, and the students were all second-generation Chinese. As everyone's families spoke Mandarin at home, the textbooks used by the school were the same as the ones in China.

Compared with these students, my level of Mandarin was inadequate for my age. Before moving to Auckland we had no access to a Chinese language school, and I resisted being taught at home. The school assessed me to be at Elementary Second Grade, and I joined a class with seven- and eight-year-olds. I was already upset that I had to give up my Saturday mornings for this class, and being put in a class with young children compounded my annoyance. After about six months, I threw a tantrum and refused to continue going.

Cynthia became my best friend that year. She was tall and laughed easily. Her time was split between her mum's house and her grandma's house, depending on her mum's work schedule.

I constantly tied up our phoneline calling her at these two houses. Her grandma could only understand Cantonese, but she came to recognise my voice. As soon as she heard it she would either shout for Cynthia, or hang up abruptly.

On the weekends, Cynthia went to the same Chinese school I had dropped out from. My parents took the opportunity to talk me into going to lessons again. I agreed, on the condition that I went to the same classes as Cynthia. Her class was at Elementary Fourth Grade, and the homework each week was much more stroke-intensive than my previous class. Occasionally her mother would drive both of us to Mandarin class. On those days, we would always arrive late.

*Fiji*

Before Kimberley, I didn't know Indian people lived in Fiji as well as in India. She had family in both, but was closer to her relatives in Fiji.

"My grandma in Fiji is the only person in my family who understands me," she sighed on the phone. Vodafone had just released a six-dollar-per-month "Best Mate" plan, and I was her Best Mate. We had a complex system between each other and our boyfriends, where we would Best Mate and be Best Mated by different people.

For Christmas, Kimberley's family were going back to Fiji. Her grandma's health was steadily declining. Each trip held the possibility that it would be the last time they'd see her.

"She's the only person in my family who appreciates the creative stuff that I do," Kimberley continued. Our parents shared similar expectations of us, the first generation to grow up here. And our parents both dismissed our naturally creative interests; they saw them as hobbies that didn't lead anywhere. As teenagers we huffed and rolled our eyes at our parents.

They didn't *understand* us. We were defined by our tastes in music and film, by seventies punk rock and Stanley Kubrick. These things were so *important* to us.

*Georgia*

Kimberley and Aidan grew up together. Their mothers worked as nurses in the same hospital ward and they'd had Kimberley and Aidan only a few months apart. As children they passed days biking up and down the sloped driveway to Kimberley's house. Nine-year-old Kimberley fell off her bike and grazed her knee. As she began to cry Aidan rushed to her, and tenderly kissed her and soothed her tears.

Kimberley texted me this story of her first kiss late at night. We were fourteen and I'd had my first kiss a few months before, with a neighbourhood boy. I had been expecting wetness, but his mouth was also slimy and sour. I wished for an experience more like hers, a movie-like romance.

As Kimberley and I texted back and forth, I learned that Aidan's family moved to the States when he was eleven, to Georgia. She'd last seen him when they visited two Christmases ago, when she and Aidan were thirteen. Aidan was allowed to stay in Kimberley's room, because her parents assumed it was an innocent childhood friendship. "Every night he would sleep in my bed and then jump onto his mattress on the floor before my parents came to check on us in the morning," she typed to me.

Kimberley talked to Aidan and me about each other constantly. I knew the names of all Aidan's siblings, that his bedroom was on the top floor of their house, and that he'd been in some trouble at school lately. We were Kimberley's two best friends. Naturally, Aidan and I started chatting on MSN Messenger. He had an interesting way of typing, omitting the "e" at the end of "the".

How's it going?

Fine
Stuck inside cos I broke
my leg tho

Oh, how'd that happen?

Jumped off th roof

Why did you do that?

Dunno
Felt like it

I didn't know what to make of Aidan. I knew a lot about him, but I had no sense of his character. Talking online gave everything a flatness. Having never met him in person, I couldn't pick which of the things he said were in jest and which were true. At first I thought he was a bit eccentric, but as time passed the content of our chats morphed from odd into outlandish. I put it down to boredom. Perhaps this was his version of fun, inventing stories to tell to people on the other side of the globe.

It seemed like Kimberley and I were the only people he talked to. His broken leg confined him indoors, and he stayed up till weird hours so he could catch the New Zealand time zone. He seemed unwell—it wasn't just the leg. He had something that I didn't have the words for. I watched my screen as I received nonsense sentences from him, not knowing what to say back.

Kimberly was worried about Aidan. She became withdrawn, even from me. She told me he was sick, but wouldn't give any details if I pressed for them. It drained her energy to spend so much time talking to him. But he was her best friend and she wanted to help him. It was what best friends did.

*Hataitai*

My belongings are packed into boxes. Tomorrow I'm leaving the country; I'll be away for six months at least. The boxes are going back to my parents' house. There is one box that holds handwritten tokens from friends. I started keeping it when I was twelve. It contains over ten years' worth of letters, birthday cards, games of exquisite corpse.

A lot of the letters are from Kimberley. We used to write a lot, as well as text and talk online. Our communication was unbroken. Each envelope contains at least ten handwritten pages, and the outsides of the A4 envelopes are decorated with illustrations.

I admire the penmanship, the effort of the craft, but I try not to read them. Too many unanswered questions. There was a time when I felt strongly that I needed answers. When Kimberley and I renewed contact in our early twenties, on one trip to Auckland I thought, *This is it. This time we're going to talk through the events of our teenage years.* But I couldn't do it. I couldn't figure out how to frame the conversation without turning it into a confrontation. I was afraid that if I started digging at the past, the tone of our friendship would regress back to a teenage state.

I'm comforted by knowing the box exists, even though I don't look in it very often. All of our digital conversations are stuttering memories, but these letters are a firm record. Maybe I can use them to excavate the truth somehow, draw evidence to support a timeline of events. But what resolution would I be looking for?

I flip through a teenage diary and feel embarrassed by the raw angst on the page. I must have felt these words at the time, but I can't connect to them anymore. I can only access them through the narrative that I've built around them. In a way, all my memories from that time are manufactured. The further I get from my teenage self, the more it feels like make-believe. There is no neat line of events, no tidy cause-and-effect to rationalise what happened. Who does it help to know if some events actually took place? The effects were real, and those were the blocks that the story was built on.

## Internet

Aidan stopped signing in on MSN Messenger. Kimberley brought his absence to my attention. She pressed me for details about our last communication, but he hadn't made sense for the last few weeks. He was talking about hearing creatures. I couldn't tell what was real and what was in his imagination. Eventually, Kimberley got hold of his younger brother. He told her that Aidan had committed suicide.

I didn't know what to say to her, and there wasn't much I could do from Whanganui. I read back through my chat history with Aidan on MSN Messenger, looking for a hidden intent, but there was nothing.

The funeral was held three days later. Kimberley couldn't be there, but Aidan's brother told her that at the service there were roses in black and red, his two favourite colours. I sat alone in my bedroom, willing more details to appear in the gaps between the words Kimberley gave me.

## Jaunt in the Chelsea Hotel

Kimberley was obsessed with the Sex Pistols, and in particular with the story of Sid Vicious and Nancy Spungen. The story of their hedonistic life together—drugs, sex and ultimately dying young—held glory and mystique. We framed their abusive relationship as an exemplar of love, and the drug abuse as synonymous with creativity.

Sid and Nancy's story ended in tragedy. After Sid was kicked off the Sex Pistols' tour for being too drug-fucked, Sid and Nancy holed up together in the Chelsea Hotel in New York City. Their room was frequented by drug dealers. A night of fighting and using heroin ended with Nancy dead in the bathroom, and Sid unable to remember who had administered the fatal stab to her stomach. Although at first he said it had been him, later he denied it. Ten days after her death, he was hospitalised for a suicide attempt. At the hospital, he tried to jump out of a window, shouting, "I want to be with my Nancy!"

The stabbing could have been an act of rage by Sid, or it could have been part of a suicide pact. Either way, he was charged for Nancy's murder. But the case never made it to court. Four months later, Sid died of a drug overdose. He and Nancy had both died young, Sid when he was twenty-one and Nancy when she was twenty. It was a repeated refrain of Nancy's that she would die before she turned twenty-one.

For Kimberley, the story of Sid and Nancy was a fitting corollary for her and Aidan. She would debate with me over who was Sid and who was Nancy. Had she led Aidan astray, like Nancy had with Sid? Or, because she played the bass guitar, was she Sid?

As we constructed these fables from our lives, I sensed the melodrama in what we were doing. But I felt I had to play along. Aidan had died first, so I agreed that he was Nancy. I worried about how seriously Kimberley took the parallels and whether, as Sid, she would decide to follow her Nancy.

## Kirikiriroa

Kimberley called me on Christmas Eve in 2013 to say that she was engaged to Reese. I was one of the first people she told outside her immediate family. This closeness flattered me.

I received an invite in the mail six months later. The venue of the wedding was in Waitakere, an hour out of Auckland. The invite list was mostly family, with a small handful of friends. I wondered how I would get there. I only knew one other person going, but they were in the wedding party and would be travelling with them.

I asked Kimberley if there was someone in her family I could get a ride with. She didn't know. They'd have lots of things to do on the day. I thought for a while. I asked if I could have a plus one, so I wasn't showing up alone to a wedding where I knew hardly anyone. She said invites were tight because they had so many family members. If they had any spare spots, they would have invited more friends.

At twenty-five, Kimberley wasn't the first person in our old friend group to get married. Our lives had diverged since I had moved away from Auckland. Marriage wasn't remotely on my radar; I had just broken up with my long-term boyfriend and moved back to the North Island. I couldn't imagine the person I would have been if I had stayed. Or maybe, regardless of location, I still would have drifted away from Kimberley.

I didn't end up going to the wedding. Weddings weren't something I placed much significance on. I figured the bride and groom would be busy and it wouldn't be a good time to catch up. I told them there'd be other chances for us to see one another.

After the wedding, they moved to Hamilton because Reese's dream job was there. After living in Auckland, they were surprised by the low house prices in the regions. It was so cheap that their parents pulled together and bought them a three-bedroom place by the river. Soon they got a puppy.

I've seen Kimberley once since her wedding day. I can't

reconcile the people we were back then with the people we are now. There she is, married and living in Hamilton. Instagramming their dog and decorating cakes with fondant roses. As a teenager I had thought that stability was boring, but I grew up and found it was a necessary side effect of my interior self settling. I hoped that this was what Kimberley had found too.

Before she got married, Kimberley told me that there were things from her past that Reese didn't know. Experiences that only we shared. It was the closest we ever got to acknowledging the intensity of our teenage friendship. When she spoke about it, her tone was even. There was no trace of accusation or discontent. I nodded, but didn't pursue the conversation. It felt like we had both reconciled with the past in ways that didn't involve each other. I looked at her, and saw that she was happy now.

### Letters from Mt Roskill

In a letter, Kimberley said she had scratched up her left arm with razorblades. As the days got hotter she kept wearing long thermals under her school blouse. Her bare-armed friends pulled at the frayed fringe of her sleeve, asking why. Kimberley was friends with two of my old friends, Cynthia and Amy. I wanted them to help her, but she didn't trust them enough. In one letter to me, she included a pseudo-psychological assessment of their personalities.

"Cynthia is avoidant. I think she has unresolved issues with her father in China. She doesn't tell us anything about him, even though she must have seen him when they last went back. I wonder if it's to do with her mother."

"Amy is so normal. She's so quiet and obedient, never wants to rock the boat, always goes along with what everyone else wants to do. I think she'll crack one day."

I wondered what she would say about me—if she saw me as naturally empathetic, if she was aware that her actions towards me could be manipulative. I imagined her assessment: "Rose is the only one who cares about me. She's trying, but she can only do so much from Whanganui. I think she'd be happier if her family had stayed in Auckland."

Or was it something like: "Rose is gullible. She believes everything that I say to her. I should watch out for Cynthia's influence on her, though. They used to be close, and I know Cynthia isn't as susceptible as Rose is."

*Main stage*

Delia invites me to a show at BATS Theatre. It starts at nine, late for a weeknight. The set is sparse and dimly lit. A microphone dangles from the roof, just above the performers' heads.

It's a two-person cast. They are friends. Best friends. Each with their issues, struggling to get through uni. They rely on each other. One girl asks the other, "If I called you, if I called you and I really needed you at 2am, would you pick up?"

"If you really needed me, I would."

The show leaves me feeling groggy. Delia and I step out into a blast of winter air. We stand in the awning outside, discussing the show.

"It reminded me of the friendships I used to have when I was younger."

"Yeah, me too. They'd always be so intense."

"Yeah! Unsustainable."

I'm standing with my arms folded, hands tucked into my armpits. Kimberley crosses my mind. I wonder what she's doing right now.

Delia yawns. "Well, I'm gonna head off. See you later!"

We hug goodbye and she walks across the street. I unlock my bicycle. In the past this moment would have turned into a longer discussion. But it's cold and late and we both have work tomorrow. Sometimes I wish for more late-night conversations in my life, but I've realised I need them less. I no longer felt the urgency to make sense of formative events in my life. My life is at a point of stability, and when I tell people stories, the events are already distant from me.

## National Women's Hospital

There was no way for me to know how Kimberley was doing unless she told me. A pause in our texting was impossible to decipher. Was she asleep? Was she ignoring me? I rode out the absences in her communication, but she would get upset if I didn't respond to her immediately. Every night she demanded I stay up texting her until she was ready to sleep, often until three or four in the morning. Her tactics to keep me up became more elaborate.

The first time was scary. I told her I couldn't stay up, and she replied, "Fine. I'll just take some pills and draw a bath and slip away. This way I won't be your problem anymore." It shook me. I sent a flurry of messages, but there was no response. It was a time before "read" receipts were invented and well before social media platforms enabled snooping on someone's "last active" status. Eventually, I fell into an uneasy sleep.

I woke at six-thirty for work and read her messages again. I decided to call her house. Kimberley's mother picked up.

"Kimberley is asleep," she said. She was a nurse at the National Women's Hospital. I didn't know why I was the one taking care of her daughter when she was the one with the medical experience. She asked if I wanted to pass on a message.

I dawdled on the line. Should I have told her about Kimberley's last text to me? It seemed too dramatic, especially now that I knew Kimberley hadn't gone through with her threat.

She texted me later that day, happy that I had called. It was proof that I still cared about her. I'd recently started a part-time job at the Mad Butcher. My shift was from 7am until 7pm on a Sunday, and I found it hard to stay up late for her. I wasn't around as much, and she took that as a sign that I was abandoning her.

The following weekend, the same thing happened. And the weekend after that. And the next one. I began to carry around a low level of dread. There were only so many times I could react with urgency after a suicide threat. After six months, her words lost all meaning. The care I was able to muster for her was a slowly deflating balloon. I was exhausted and needed it to stop, for her sake as well as mine.

*Onehunga*

Cynthia was my best friend when I left Auckland, not Kimberley. But we didn't keep in touch in the same way. Cynthia and Kimberley stayed in the same friend group all through high school. I wonder if Cynthia ever felt hurt that Kimberley became my best friend instead. But it would have been weird to talk about our relationship, because we were just friends.

I asked Cynthia for help when Kimberley's cutting became more frequent. Being so far away from everyone, I didn't know what I could do. Cynthia knew a little about the situation, but not as much as I did, and she didn't have much sympathy for Kimberley. Cynthia had always seemed self-absorbed to me.

U know, I dunno if she's
telling the truth about all this

What?

Like with Aidan, and Max
and all those people. They're
all from out of town. None
of us have ever met them, I'm
not sure if they're real.

Really? Doesn't Max
live in Onehunga?

I dunno. I've never met him.
I think she just does it for the
attention

Hmm

*Pick-up zone*

I was thirteen when my grandparents went back to China. They
spent a couple of years in Chóngmíng, and returned to New
Zealand when I was fifteen. When they arrived, they needed
to transfer between the international and domestic terminals
at Auckland Airport. With no English, it was impossible for
them to find their way on their own. My parents had the dairy
to run, so they sent me to Auckland for the day to chaperone
them from one side of the airport to the other.

Kimberley and I had been talking about me coming to
Auckland too. She didn't want to go to the doctor without
me. We thought about waiting for summer break, but it felt
more urgent. Over the last month I had become sluggish, and
didn't have the energy to enjoy anything. Kimberley's texts,
whether good or bad, kept me constantly on edge. I needed her
to rely on other people. This opportunity presented itself, and
she agreed to book a doctor's appointment in the four-hour gap
between my grandparents' connecting flights. I couldn't cope
with the amount of support she demanded from me.

I flew up to Auckland and strolled the short distance between the domestic and international terminals. It was a balmy day. I waited outside the arrivals gate, checking my phone. My grandparents arrived in heavy coats, having left a frosty winter. My bu'uah was in much worse shape than I'd expected. She suffered from travel sickness, but this time it was unusually severe. Her pocket was stuffed with plastic bags.

Kimberley and her mother arrived at the international pick-up zone. My grandparents and I got into their car. My bu'uah knocked on the window, asking for it to be wound down. In the short drive to the domestic terminal, she filled up a plastic bag with vomit.

I had planned to take my grandparents with us to the doctor, but given my grandma's state I knew it was a bad idea. Kimberley's mum stayed in the drop-off zone while Kimberley followed my grandparents and me into the domestic terminal. I found a place for them to sit and wait.

Kimberley was impatient to leave. "Let's go now. My mum's waiting."

Anything I said to my grandparents would be inadequate at this point. My bu'uah was leaning back with her eyes closed, plastic bag clutched in her hand. I said to my kon-kon, lamely, "Ng nyau gin 'ng ban-nyoe tsuaeh." | "I have to go with my friend."

"Pei! Ki lar-di! 'Ng kue bu'uah!" | "Pei! Why are you going? Just look at Bu'uah!"

"'Ng nyau ki. Tson nyau 'ngi." | "I need to go. It's important."

"Bu'uah 'ngeh? Ueh tseh!" | "What if something happens to Bu'uah? You can't leave us here!"

Even if I was fluent in Chóngmíng dialect, there would have been no adequate excuse for leaving them alone in the airport.

In the doctor's office, Kimberley's mum and I sat with her through her appointment. The doctor asked Kimberley a series of questions and she responded with a number from one to five, indicating how strongly she associated with the statement, or how bad she had been feeling. The doctor asked how long she'd felt depressed, and she burst into tears. He handed her a box of tissues. "Since Nani died," she said into her hands. Her grandmother had died recently. The funeral had been held in Suva one month ago. Kimberley had sent me five dollars' worth of texts charged at the international rate of eighty cents per 160 characters.

During the appointment, there was no mention of Aidan. The two deaths had happened in such quick succession, maybe for Kimberley they had spiralled and merged like a pair of black holes. This was one of many details that I thought was glossed over or unexplained. It didn't fit my understanding of Kimberley's situation. As the doctor asked his prescriptive questions, and Kimberley filtered her answers in front of her mum, I felt a growing dissonance. But I sat in my plastic chair, letting myself feel a trickle of relief. Now that she was getting help, the load would be taken off me. I wished I could have explained this to my grandparents.

Back at the airport, my grandma and grandpa hadn't moved from the seats where I had left them. We caught our return flight, no trouble, and my mum met us at Whanganui Airport. But, of course, my kon-kon told my mother that I had abandoned them at the airport and gone off with my friend. I had known it wasn't the right thing to do. But there was no right thing to do. All of my choices were bad for someone.

"你怎么可以把爷爷奶奶留在机场呢!" | "How could you leave your kon-kon and bu'uah at the airport like that!" my mum yelled at me. What could I say? She didn't know the relationship that Kimberley and I had. Our closeness, our codependence, the deep knowledge of each other that our parents couldn't have. I lacked the words to describe the shape or form of her illness, and how scared and tired it made me feel. I stared back in stony silence at her, unable to explain my actions.

*Quiet office*

In her last six months in Wellington, Viv lived in the upper flat of a broad wooden house in Newtown. Her house was around the corner from mine. It was the closest we had ever lived to each other. In the past we would travel as far as from Lyall Bay to Brooklyn to see each other.

We had an understanding that when you were meeting at someone's house for dinner, you didn't have to bring something. Our dinners together were frequent enough that you'd just cook next time. There was no veneer of politeness or an expectation of being "on" when we hung out.

The last time I saw Viv, we had dinner at her house. She was cooking a hodge-podge meal composed of a single pork chop, three sausages, kale, and rice cooked in coconut cream.

Goodbyes used to have much more gravity when I was younger. We would send messages like "afk" or "brb". Now there was a continuous stream of conversation that spanned various platforms. Viv and I were saying goodbye, but in some ways it was just a shift in our primary medium of communication.

Viv's replacement flatmate had already begun moving in. A double mattress was propped up against the lounge wall and black rubbish bags of clothes were littered through the house. I almost kicked over a bright green bowl with a flowery spout. A trickling sound came from it. Bending down, I saw that the flower at the centre was dispensing water.

"What the hell is that?" I asked.

"Oh, Stacey has a cat. Apparently it can't drink still water." She looked at me and shrugged. I pulled a face. She waggled her eyebrows and we burst into laughter. Sometimes a look could set us off. For a time we worked in the same coworking place and would laugh uproariously in the communal kitchen. The kitchen was shared with a group of uptight middle-aged women, and they would come in and shush us like we were children. "This is a kitchen, not a café." Viv and I would stifle our laughter behind our hands until they left, wondering what had gone so wrong in their lives that they had forgotten how to share a laugh with a friend.

## Remuera

On the doctor's recommendation, Kimberley was referred to a specialist youth mental health clinic. Her mother didn't want her to go on medication. Every week they drove out to see the psychologist in Remuera.

I wanted this to change her condition immediately. It didn't, but at least I wasn't her lifeline anymore. Something in my mum's anger over the airport incident stayed with me. I started reconsidering how much support I needed to provide, now that she had access to professional help.

I talked to my boyfriend Callum about it. "She's using you as an emotional sponge," he said. No one had been so direct to me about it before. I knew that Cynthia thought it was all attention-seeking, but it had felt different to me. I had spent so many nights listening to her troubles.

Before Kimberley started counselling, we had the idea to start a joint journal in place of the letters that we normally wrote. I bought a notebook and started it off, writing entries over a week and then posting it to her. In the time that she had the notebook, things started to sour between us. I didn't have the same patience with her as before. Now that she had a psychologist, I didn't want to stay up with her anymore. There was never a good time to broach the subject, and my words came, too harsh, one tired night.

The week after, the notebook arrived in the mail. She had hardly written anything, but several of the pages were streaked with blood.

*Service centre*

I started volunteering for Youthline when I was twenty-four. They had an intensive six-month training programme. We were taught the basics of person-centred counselling, and progressed through modules on eating disorders, grief, relationships and the like. People from NGOs and charities in the social sector ran sessions for their area of expertise. I thought ruefully of my younger self, who would have benefited from those services. Back then I had no idea they existed, let alone what they did.

The guilt I felt for not continuing to support Kimberley stayed with me for a long time. It was never clear to me how sincerely she meant her threats of suicide, but each time I would mentally prepare for the worst. Even when it didn't eventuate, I preferred the relief of being over-cautious. After I cut off contact with her, I continued to check up on her surreptitiously through our mutual friends. As time passed, I trusted that she would continue to get better. It wasn't my job to look out for her anymore.

Learning the basics of counselling at Youthline reassured me that I had done what I could in our teenage years. After the training programme, I understood that I was far from equipped to handle a crisis situation even now, let alone back then. If a caller presented as an immediate danger to themselves, we were advised to call the Crisis Assessment Treatment Team.

As a teenager, I had been in way over my head. I was still getting to grips with my own emotional state and was in no position to carry someone else. Some of my attempts to help Kimberley hadn't been constructive—platitudes like, "Think of people who have it much worse than you!" or "Just try to be happier." It astounds me that we both came out of that experience relatively unscathed.

## The Octagon

Max was a friend of Aidan's. At first, Kimberley only saw Max when she bought weed off him, but after Aidan died they started hanging out more and eventually got together. Max was three years older than us. Back then, none of these things were red flags. Not the drug dealing, not the power imbalance that can come with an age gap. We were so desperate to grow up, it was a mark of maturity to be involved in things that were off-limits.

Kimberley would tell me about sneaking Max into her room at night, or sneaking out to see him. She would hint about substances harder than weed and I clung on to these details, partly out of concern for her wellbeing, partly out of fascination. Her life was much more interesting than mine.

Max moved to Dunedin to attend Otago University and their relationship became long distance. One school holidays, she flew down from Auckland to visit him. By then it was winter. She told me about strolling through the Octagon, seeing snow for the first time. Max lived in a flat and skipped lectures to hang out with her. Except when they were watching a movie, or sleeping, she would be texting me an account of her day.

I took some pills

                                    How many

Dunno. A few

                         How many is a few

Didn't count

                           What sorta pills

Dunno.
Max's flatmate has a
ginger cat, Ziggy

                                  Cool, is it cute

Yeah

I don't know if they officially broke up, or if their relationship petered out. As she became more withdrawn and downcast, she stopped talking about him as much. I got the sense that, for one reason or another, he wasn't a good support to her.

## Universal Resource Locator

The main online platform that Kimberley, Aidan and I used was MSN Messenger, and later Bebo. Neither of these exist anymore, and they aren't archived. At one stage I had downloaded my chat history with Kimberley, but that was on an old computer. Every electronic record of that time is gone.

In my early twenties, I still thought about these events regularly. There were times when Cynthia's words really got into my head. What if Kimberley had made it all up? What if Aidan had never existed, and Kimberley had set up a fake account for him online? The deception wouldn't have been hard.

I went on Kimberley's Facebook page and scrolled through her friends list. I searched for "Max". Nothing. I tried the names of other mutuals of Aidan and Kimberley, but I couldn't find the right people. By this stage, it was too late to prove anything. Aidan had died before Facebook was ubiquitous, and, besides, many people chose not to friend people from their early high-school years. I wished I could remember Aidan's brother's name, or their family name.

Black roses. This detail from Kimberley about Aidan's funeral came back to me. I had never seen black roses. I googled "do black roses exist". Several photoshopped images come up, but none of naturally occurring colour. One florist said that it was possible to dye the petals. As with everything else, it was inconclusive.

*Video store*

I liked to rent DVDs where the plotline involved a conflict between two best friends. One of the two friends would do something that changed the other's perception of their character. At the time, I found it unrealistic. How could you not know *everything* about your best friend? My life was short enough that my best friend Kimberley and I knew everything about each other.

It was the first genuine relationship in my life. We were old enough to have complex feelings, both in our individual lives and in the interactions we had together. Our relationship was where I learned how to care for someone. It was different from the care that I received from my parents, or the care I gave to my brother. Those relationships had been established at birth, whereas Kimberley and I could have picked any other person as a best friend. It wasn't even a friendship of convenience or circumstance. There was no reason that we needed to talk to each other every day. But being chosen and needed was an intermission from my otherwise boring and isolated life in Whanganui.

Kimberley and I would tell each other that we loved each other. The words expressed the same reverence as they did in my romantic relationships, as our friendship had the same emotional intensity, if not more. Perhaps this was unusual for teenagers at that time, to express love when there was no romance or sex involved. Usually, with a first love, the three go together. My friendship with Kimberley flattened out the hierarchies I'd learned about relationships.

But we were just friends. When we stopped talking, there were no guidelines for processing the break-up. There were no milestones I could point to, like meeting each other's families or the number of years we'd spent together, that would help to explain the significance of the separation. An ambiguity is present in the definition of "a friend". The word is large enough to encompass relationships with daily or yearly contact.

No other relationship I've had since has approached the same ferocity, but I've learned that intimacy isn't built solely on reliance. As teenagers we traded secrets as currency for love, cupping parts of each other in clumsy hands.

*Whanganui*
Kimberley is texting me. She doesn't want me to sleep, to leave her alone with herself. She doesn't understand why I can't stay up with her anymore. My phone buzzes.

Don't you care about
me anymore

> I do, I just have
> work tomorrow

Stay up with me until
I fall asleep

Things aren't the same as before. She suggests playing the alphabet game, and picks colours as the category. I close my eyes between turns.

The buzz of my phone interrupts the darkness. I squint at her latest message. It says "Lavender". Okay. "M". A colour that starts with "m". I flip the screen facedown while I think.

My phone vibrates in my hand. I've dozed off. I open the message. She's sent me a blank text. It's her way of waking me up. I receive another one. Sighing, I close my eyes again. An incorporeal red square materialises behind my eyes. It reminds me of the ignored texts.

More muted buzzes plague my sleep. I can't do it. I just can't do it anymore. I don't want to finish the game.

# FIVE–FIVE

The thing about walking is that it's not quite enough exercise to block your thoughts. Walking uphill is, but not on a flat path like this. You're making an effort to walk faster. This burns up some mental focus. But there's still too much space inside your head. It's just you and your thoughts, and the day has barely started.

You lift your chin in the crisp air. Not a single cloud. Powder-blue mountains, slate beneath your feet, ahead the milky trail—normally pale colours pop at this altitude. Everything is oversaturated, like looking through a new glasses prescription.

As is common when you are alone for long periods of time, you have lost your grasp on the motivations behind your choices. You haven't been alone for that long, not really. Only a few days. You started the track alone when you were in Besishahar and thought nothing of being alone. You knew you'd find people in a few days, and you did.

You met Mia by a rickety teahouse overlooking a waterfall. You had put down your pack and bush-bashed a path down to the bottom of the waterfall. It was louder than you expected, and mist settled on your glasses. When you re-emerged, hands brown from clutching dirt, Mia was there, admiring the view. She was also alone.

You remind yourself that you like walking. Today you've been walking for about three hours. Not that long. You think of some of the longest days you've spent hiking in New Zealand. Those days would have been ten, maybe twelve hours. Stops for lunch, morning tea and afternoon tea. Not truly continuous. Your bum would rest on damp moss or on a hut porch if you'd planned it right, but not for long. There was a lot of ground to cover in a day. You didn't want to be on the track after the sun had set. And you knew your feet would start hurting at the seven-hour mark. But invariably, on those ten- or twelve-hour days, you'd end up walking in the dark.

Walking in the dark was bad news. In the dim light, your pace halved. Your head torch didn't help much. Track markers became harder to spot, cairns almost impossible. The last few hours were always misery, but you knew better than to complain. It wouldn't get you to where you needed to be any faster. And as your Outward Bound instructor said to you once, "You can be cold, wet and miserable. Or you can be cold and wet."

At the time, you found the platitude corny and predictable. You still do. But, somehow, the words always pop back up in your memory when you're having a crappy time. Right now you're neither cold nor wet, but you're still trying to fight away the miserable.

Two men are coming your way. They wear khaki pants and matching green and orange jackets. You have seen countless hikers dressed in this garb. As you pass one another you say hello.

Even though you're in Nepal, the English greeting is the default. You think: *I haven't seen many hikers today.* There's another case of globalism. Even in your head you've stopped calling people on the track "trampers". The word has been trained out of you, because no one understood you when you used it.

Mia sure didn't. For the most part you understood each other, but there were a lot of things you two couldn't say. At least she spoke English; you didn't know a word of German. As the elevation got higher, the water you drank became bitter and more speckled with white flakes. "Ugly water," she had called it, wincing it down.

Two days ago you were sitting on a stone wall drinking the ugly water and watching Mia make up her mind. She was talking to Ben, a cocky lad with a cotton-top tamarin hairdo. You two first met him at Tilicho Lake; over dinner he bragged about the number of pills he took at raves in his hometown of Manchester. Then he started giving preposterous hiking tips. "You've got to link arms when you go over the pass, you know what I mean?" You resisted the urge to roll your eyes, but Mia mistook his confidence for authority. She had been getting steadily more anxious as the pass approached.

Ben and his guide were heading to the next town. Mia was shifting from foot to foot, looking between you and Ben. You had another mouthful of water. It felt like swallowing rocks, and your throat was tight from inflammation. It was three in the afternoon and you had had enough for the day. Going on in your state felt like an unnecessary risk. There were at least ten more walking days ahead.

Mia was anxious to keep a steady pace, and it didn't look like you could help her. If anything, you were slowing her down. And she had further to go than you. She had planned to go up to Base Camp as well. You would have split up eventually. But this was sooner than you'd expected, and, given your physical and financial condition, you felt like Mia was being heartless. What did she owe you, though? Nothing.

Mia shook hands with Ben and they smiled at each other. Her mind was made up. She walked over to you, looking mildly apologetic. "I'm going to go with them," she said, jerking her head back.

"Okay," you replied.

Her lips pressed out a smile, and she embraced you stiffly. "See you in New Zealand?"

"Sure," you replied. You never accepted her Facebook friend request.

You spot the man with the beard again. It's wiry and long, down to his navel. Mr Big Beard has been sporadically appearing and disappearing in your field of vision. Today's route has wound its way along the side of a valley. The mountainsides are stark. It's been at least three days since you saw green vegetation. The colours of caramel, cinnamon bark and leather surround you.

Your throat still hurts. It doesn't burn like it did two days ago, and the feverish feeling is gone from your chest, your head. But you're still not a hundred per cent better. What was that rating thing they used to do on Outward Bound? Out of five. On each hand you'd hold up your fingers, from one to five, to show how you were feeling. Left hand for physical health, right hand for mental health. No matter how hard things got, everyone was always a five–five. The girl who got shin splints: five–five. The girl who had her achilles tendonitis flare up: five–five. You think of your throat. It's not that bad, really. You're a five–five. You just didn't expect to feel so abandoned. It's a funny alliance, that of a travelling companion. Even though you didn't know Mia that well, you'd thought there was an unspoken agreement that you'd stick together. But you don't know where she is now, and it's unlikely you'll see her again.

You think about the cash you have left. Two, maybe three thousand Nepalese rupees—it's not enough. The cost of dahl baat keeps rising with the altitude. It's tripled in price. You paid 850 rupees for the dahl baat last night. Even so, it was barely seven New Zealand dollars. You have the money sitting in your bank account, but you can't access it. The nearest ATM is two days' walk away, in Jonsom. When you set out, you knew that you needed enough money for at least the first fourteen days. But you miscalculated. How were you to know that the ATMs had such low limits on the amount of cash you could withdraw at once? And that they went out of order so often? You did the maths at the start and thought it would be okay. It would be tight, but it would be okay. But you hadn't counted on getting sick.

Thorong Phedi. This is where Mia was heading the day she left you. You see a single teahouse, long and rectangular. It has a flat metal roof and is built with bricks the colour of river crabs. At the higher altitudes there are fewer teahouses. When you started the track, each township had at least five. To charm you into business, they were all painted bright colours. Alternating green and white bricks, purple door, orange window frames and pink eaves.

You stop and go inside the drab teahouse. You have no money to spend, but sitting is free. Mr Big Beard is there, and he smiles at you.

You sit opposite him. Immediately he starts talking. American.

The cursory "on the track" questions are asked. Nationality, where you started from today, where you're headed. His answers surprise you.

131

"That's quite some distance you're covering today."

"Well, I'm actually on my second lap," he says. "I did the first one much faster. It was a charity fundraiser. We were trying to break the Guinness World Record."

You learn that he had been in the US Army when he suffered debilitating injuries and was told that he would never walk again. He describes his gruelling recovery process—a montage of him struggling, hobbling, then triumphantly striding. Now he's a professional walker. He gets paid to do incredible thru-hikes around the world. He's done the Pacific Crest Trail a number of times, and he plans to do the Te Araroa track in the near future. This comparatively brief hike, over fourteen to twenty-four days, is his idea of a holiday, a charity run in between the paid gigs.

He's well practised in telling his story, and, despite your resistance to the obvious emotional manipulation, it still has an effect on you. A plate of food arrives at the table. Burger and chips. He cuts it in half, gestures at you to take a portion. It's the most generosity you've been shown from a fellow tourist since you landed in Nepal.

You feel compelled to share a bit about yourself. You tell him about your walking buddy abandoning you when she knew you were sick and that you were running out of money. Like the majority of the people on the track, the Annapurna Circuit was Mia's first experience of a multi-day tramp. Her naïvety had astounded you.

In hindsight, you weren't ready to leave China for Nepal when you did. You'd just reached a place with the language, the systems and the culture not to feel like a complete tourist; you were finally able to have conversations that weren't superficial. But you had to leave. It was a condition of the double-entry tourist visa you were on.

You thought you would be excited to speak in English again. Using Mandarin all day made you so tired. English was easy, effortless. Then you arrived at the hostel in Kathmandu and realised that everyone was a young, white traveller seeking a picture-perfect experience. In their conversations they congratulated themselves for being so brave and inspiring to take on such an adventure. You thought of your conversations with Chinese people about going overseas, about how hard it was to get even a tourist visa. Travelling wasn't a rite of passage in China; it was a privilege. You held your tongue.

Before your time in China you'd never noticed how often English speakers talked about themselves. I, I, I, over and over again. "I came to Nepal 'cause I heard it was cheap, and then I found out that everyone comes here for hikes, so, like, I decided to do one too! My friends think it's so funny, like, it's so *me* to do something crazy like this. I've only ever walked for, like, three hours before."

Mr Big Beard agrees with you about the inexperience of the other hikers. He's noticed it too. "But you know what you're doing," he says. "You've been making a good pace today, I've seen you on the track. It seems like the solution to your problems is just to go over the pass today. Why not? It's only 10am. You'll have plenty of time."

You pause. "Is there any snow up there?"

"No, there shouldn't be. I was there only a week or so ago."

"What about the wind? Everyone talks about getting through the pass before ten in the morning because that's when the wind picks up. But how bad can the wind actually be?"

He looks at you and shrugs, because you've already answered your own question. "I think you'll be fine."

For the first time in the last three days, you think, *I'll be fine*. You're surprised that you've been swept up by the collective anxiety of the first-time hikers. None of them knew what they were doing. They started the track wearing new, knock-off boots. They listened to their porters and guides, who made the most conservative decisions possible.

Recommendations for getting through the pass usually go like this: If you start from High Camp you'll need to leave by 6am; if you're leaving from Thorong Phedi you'll need to leave by 4am. You left today from Letdar, so by that logic you should have left yesterday. But you know from adding up the times in the guidebook that going from Letdar over the pass should take eight hours. You've done half of that already and there are still seven daylight hours left.

Mr Big Beard stands up to leave. "Good luck!"

"Bye!"

You eat the last five chips.


You're higher again now. The sky has faded slightly, like you're looking at it through an Instagram filter. Trail markers have appeared, thin staffs of yellow and white. The path ahead dominates your view. In the background, a rocky mountain with a dollop of cream on top. Dirt gives away to pale silt. The colour palette is shrinking.

It wasn't the fact that she left; it was that earlier she'd been so adamant that she wouldn't. One of the first stories Mia shared with you was one of abandonment. Like you, she had come alone to Nepal. At her hostel she had found a group to walk with. Australian, British, French—they spoke English as their common language. The bus to the trailhead was uncomfortable, stuffy and three hours behind schedule. Mia realised she still needed to get her hiking permit. The others got theirs the day before. "It'll just be ten minutes, please wait!" she pleaded. But they were all anxious to get on the road, because it was their first day and they didn't want to start behind schedule. "And they just left me!" she told you. "Completely by myself!"

High Camp comes sooner than you expect. You check the time. Eleven. From here it's three, maybe four hours through the pass. Even with breaks, you'll easily clear it today. You take stock of yourself again. Five–five. Besides, what will you do if you stop here? You'll start getting cold as soon as you stop moving, and you don't have spare money for hot drinks. Best to keep moving.

You pass through the two monochromatic teahouses at this settlement. One is two-storeyed. The buildings look out of place among the peaks, built somewhere so clearly uninhabitable. No vegetation, no water source. No reason to exist except for you, and people like you, and your tourist rupees.

Mia was a much better haggler than you. The guidebooks said that most teahouse owners would waive the room charge if you ate all your meals at their establishment. But you never had the heart to ask. The room charge was only three or four New Zealand dollars. It felt rude. Before Mia came along you paid the room charge, but once you were together you got the discount because Mia always asked for it. She was watching her budget. After all, she was planning on spending an entire year abroad. Nepal was cheap, but there were more expensive destinations on her list, like New Zealand.

A shape appears at the ridge. Someone is coming the other way. From their lack of fluorescent clothing you pick them to be a local. They start to drop down the ridge, and you see that they are leading a horse. Definitely a local. Their clothes are washed-out from the sun, and open sandals are on their feet. You don't know it yet, but this is the last person you'll see for the next three hours.

The blogs you read before you came on this trip raved about the social element of the Annapurna Circuit. Many described it as a "world party", a multicultural experience where everyone was united in their love of walking. But you've only met people from Europe, Israel, North America and Australia. And one bloke from New Zealand, in his forties, with a name blokey enough that you forgot it as soon as he told you.

Some world party. But what did you expect from reading an English-language blog? When you set out you were looking for a walking partner who spoke English. You reasoned that most travellers would at least speak English as a second language. Though Mia's English wasn't actually that good. Your Mandarin was probably better than her English. But despite claims from other hikers that there are *so* many Chinese people on the track, you haven't seen a single one.

On you walk. One foot after the other foot, after the other foot. These small steps add up. Suddenly you've crossed a great distance. You're weary after the long day so far. But at any given point in time, you know you have the energy for just one more step. Just one. You can always trick yourself into it. And despite your tiredness, you walk another kilometre. It's easier if you stop willing your feet, if you let them fall into a pattern where they can keep the beat themselves.

The wind is picking up, like they said it would. You're wearing all of your layers bar one. There were so many horror stories about this ascent. The common wisdom is that six is a good number of people to cross with. The more the better. The path ahead is compacted and well marked. You don't understand why people get so worried, what the larger numbers are supposed to protect them from. If the season was different and the path was whited out by snow, you would feel differently.

Risk of altitude sickness is something you take seriously, and you and Mia spent a few days in Manang to acclimatise, as was recommended. A side trip to Lake Tilicho was next, and on the way the two of you were joined by three Nepalese men. They were childhood friends from Pokhara. They had talked about doing the circuit all through their youth, figuring that there would always be time in the future. When they entered their twenties, one moved to New York after winning the Green Card Lottery, another took over the family business, and the last went to university.

Reunited in Pokhara for the first time in years, the three of them decided to seize the opportunity and walk the circuit. Because time was short, they took a Jeep to Manang, and after one night's sleep they left the next morning. Not a good idea. They had quickly gained over 4000 metres of elevation. To be safe, they should have stayed put for at least three days.

"Are you sure you're feeling okay?" you asked them over lunch. One of them ripped open a box of Snickers bars. None of them had sensible shoes or suitable gear.

"Of course!" the Green Card winner replied, pushing the box towards you. He had the best English. "Please have one, we have three boxes."

The other two conferred in Nepalese, and the paler of the pair stood up and walked out of the dining room with his hiking pack.

"Is he okay?" you asked.

"Of course. He's just got a headache."

"That's one of the first signs of altitude sickness."

"No, it's okay, he's just going to leave his bag here and we'll pick it up again on our way back from the lake."

You didn't believe they were going to be okay. But the five of you set out again. The Green Card winner had a portable speaker. He was a DJ in America, and he played you his favourite mixes. You walked along the trail to Justin Bieber. Half an hour later, the one with the headache groaned and the music was turned off. The previously healthy two also started to complain of headaches. All three of them stopped. "We'll meet you there," they said, waving you and Mia on.

"Head back down," you urged them. "It's the only way to get better."

You wonder where they are now. Hopefully back in Pokhara. The track has started flattening out again. It weaves between two rises, one brown and the other orange and white like candy corn. Rounding the corner you see a small wooden hut, and a spectrum of coloured flags. Beside the flags a bank rises sharply, turning into striated rock and a white cap of snow.

This must be the pass. You've made it.

The gust is strong. You let your arms go and feel them flap behind you. But the peaks around you are unmoving. No swirl of dust; they are solid, static. In your photographs there will be no indication that there was anything here other than stillness.

The sign marking Thorong La Pass is entirely in English. "Congratulation for the success!!!" it tells you. A matted mass of prayer flags spreads out around the sign. Some are bright and new; others are brown and faded from repeated lashings against the ground. Up close you can hear the flags beating in the wind. A frenzied vibration, like blowflies hitting a clear pane of glass.

You take a selfie with the sign, making sure to capture the altitude in the frame. Later you'll post this on social media and receive over one hundred likes. You'll remember how miserable you were at the time, how isolated you felt at the highest point you'd ever been in your life.

\*

The way down is worse. You'd been so focussed on getting to the pass that you didn't think about the descent. Going down is harder on the knees. You wish for walking poles, even though you don't know how to use them. The brief high of the pass is over. You have to go down. The gradient shifts again. It's as steep as it was on the way up, possibly even steeper. But coming up, if you were to fall, it wouldn't be far to go before your palms hit the ground.

You have reason to be scared now.

If you get injured and can't make it to the next town, you'll be in trouble. A night outside. No shelter. Temperatures well below zero. That's what dying of exposure would be like. You wish for the safety net of a group of people. The last time you saw someone was three hours ago. It's 2pm now. You doubt you'll see anyone else on the track again today.

If you were to fall forward, the arc traced by your body would be more than ninety degrees. The ground is loamier than before; it has give. Small clouds of dust swirl around your ankles.

You try not to worry. You know that you are the biggest danger to yourself right now. One breath in. Focus on keeping your breathing level, your footsteps level. No need to be in a hurry; it's more important to stay safe.

One step after another. You don't know what's ahead. You don't know that after a few hours of cautious descent there will be an unexpected teahouse. The location isn't marked on the map. It's not the destination you need to get to today, but you will sit for a while. The owner will chat to you, invite you to stay, but you'll say you don't have enough money and will have to press on to Muktinath. You will sit for longer than you intend. You won't be able to get out of the chair. The owner will take pity on you, your wet nose, your scratchy throat.

It's the end of the day, he will say, and there are no lodgers, so he was going to go back to Muktinath anyway. You and your big bag will squeeze behind him on the scooter. The sun will set as you bump all the way along the uneven road to town. He will drop you off at a hotel owned by one of his buddies. You will rest.

When you go to check out, you will realise that they've waived the room fee. The man who dropped you off must have mentioned your money situation. You will feel ashamed. You've become that type of tourist. The freeloader. The one who feels entitled to things, the one who haggles over a pittance just to make sure they are not being "ripped off".

But you don't know this feeling yet, while you're still concentrating on the descent. In the steepest parts you walk sideways, the outside edge of your right foot testing the way. You oscillate between feeling incredibly stupid that you've taken this risk, and supremely confident that everything will be fine.

From here, you don't know that in two days, when you get on the trail again, you'll hear a ute rumbling behind you. The road will be dusty. Your nose and mouth are covered by a stretchy red and white neckerchief. You'll turn around and see three people standing on the back of the vehicle. Three sets of eyes will peer at you inquisitively. "Hi!" one of them will shout at you.

As their faces pass, you make out their dark hair and olive skin. The ute starts to pass you by. You want them to stop.

You call out, "你好!"

"诶!" | "Eiii!"

They scream at the driver, asking him to stop the vehicle so you can get on.

You know you have a Chinese face. You were used to

drawing attention away from it. In New Zealand, it was a bad sign when people identified you by your Chinese face. The usual question would follow. Where are you from? No, where are you actually from? Okay, but where are your parents from? You opened your New Zealand mouth to distract people from your Chinese face.

In China you just had a face. If people looked carefully, they could identify something foreign in your behaviour, your style of dress. But people didn't usually look so closely. People tend to look at the face.

In that moment, when you see their faces in the back of the ute, you will want to draw their attention to your face. The ute will stop, and one of them will lean forward, hand outstretched, in response to your face. You are happy to take it. You are happy because you have experienced so few times when your face has been recognised like this.

You take your bag off and smile at them. Two women and a man, all about your age. You try to talk over the gallop of the motor, but it's too dusty to keep your mouth open. So you look out over the dry hills, drinking in a sense of relief.

Your group will hop off in the next town at noon. You'll discuss the usual trail questions over lunch at a teahouse. They'll be excited to have a native English speaker among them; it makes communicating with the Nepalese easier. Food arrives. Spoons dip into your daal and rice. You take a steamed momo from another's plate. You've missed these little gestures. It had felt so foreign eating with Mia. She never wanted to share; she didn't care to try your meal. You had to keep firmly to the boundaries of your plate.

You will remember only one of their names: Paco. The woman from Běijīng, in a cobalt blue jacket. She is the only one of the three who has an English name. The other woman is in her early twenties, from Xiàmén. Her jacket is dusty pink. She came to Nepal through Tibet, and is surprised to hear that only 身份证, Chinese identity cardholders, are allowed free travel through the Tibetan autonomous region. The man is a photographer from Lìjiāng. He carries a bulky camera and several lenses in his backpack.

You will mention you have to get to Jonsom to go to the ATM. The photographer will slap his hand on the table.

"太好了! 我现金带多了。" | "Fantastic! I brought too much cash." He will pull out a wad of rupees and immediately start counting. "你要多少? 四万?六万?" | "How much do you need? Forty thousand? Sixty thousand?"

You will mentally tally up the numbers of days left. He will give you the cash. You'll open WeChat and transfer him the equivalent in RMB.


Your right foot flies ahead of you. The rocks grumble in unison as you fall backwards onto your bum and slide a few paces down the slope. Your heart is racing. You bring your hands up and find your palms covered in white dust. Sitting a while, you survey the ground. The soil is getting darker. You have to be more careful.

You sigh and feel sorry for yourself. What are you even doing here? Nepal, like other cheap Asian countries, is a magnet for white people trying to find themselves. You didn't come to Nepal for that. In fact, it was supposed to be a respite from the finding of yourself you were doing in China.

You miss speaking Mandarin. When you first arrived in China, you would mentally translate Mandarin speech to English, form a reply in English, then translate it to Mandarin. By the time you left for Nepal, you hadn't needed the middleman of English anymore. Mandarin felt less like a secondary language, China less like a secondary culture.

You look to the horizon. The sky is showing the faintest blush of orange. You should get moving before it gets dark. You take stock of your internal state. Five–five.

# YELLOW FEVER

1

"Are you sure?" whispered Callum.

"Yes," I replied. It was late, past midnight. We'd been fooling around for some time, our clothes kicked to the bottom of the bed. Watery light filtered through the curtains. His face was grainy in black and white. Not enough light for his freckles to be shown, not enough light for his expression to be read.

"Okay."

He reached for the packet of flavoured Durex condoms by the single pillow. He drew one out and tore it open carefully. I waited as he slid it down his penis.

He shuffled on top of me and I spread my legs. Under the covers he fumbled with our genitals, trying to find the entrance of my vagina. I reached down to guide the rubbery tip to the right place. He lowered his body down, stacking his hips on mine. My thighs rolled slightly outward and upward from the weight. I didn't expect him to feel so heavy.

He ground up against me with a stilted rhythm. I took that to mean he was in, even though I couldn't feel anything. But what was a dick inside me even supposed to feel like? I thought about asking him if he was in, but that would be rude. Besides, I was glad that it didn't hurt, and that he hadn't come instantly. He shuffled again, leaning to one side. It didn't make the motion any smoother, and my leg was getting crushed by the side of his hip.

Next, he tried propping himself up on his hands. His weight was lifted off my chest, and his pubic bone pressed against mine. That seemed to work better. He tried thrusting from one angle, and then another. Occasionally I felt an internal tug or friction from his experiments. Was it pleasurable? I guess it felt better than nothing.

We persisted with our silent thrusting for at least ten more minutes. I couldn't tell if he was enjoying it or not. He wasn't making any sounds. Did that indicate a lack of pleasure or a fear of being heard? My hips and legs started to feel sore. Was he close to coming? He would've told me if he had, right?

Callum stopped. He rolled off me carefully. We rearranged our bodies and he threw an arm across my torso.

I nestled closer to him. "Did you come?" I asked quietly.

"No," he responded.

What did that mean? Had I done something wrong? "Okay," I said, aware that the pause was held for too long.

He rested his head against mine. "I think I'm just not used to the sensation."

"Okay," I said again. He moved his head away.

I tried to gauge whether I felt different in any way. After all, Callum and I weren't virgins anymore. Did I feel differently about him now? Did I feel more adult? Was sex what I expected? I wasn't exactly picturing fireworks, but I thought there would be a more pronounced difference from the times when he'd fingered me. Actually, I probably got more out of the fingering. His penis was like a big awkward finger, incapable of performing delicate motor tasks.

The metal bedsprings wheezed as Callum shifted his weight on the single bunk. Was he trying to get to sleep? Was he thinking about what we just did? I think he was surprised when I suggested that we have sex. We had been together for six months and I'd known friends who'd only waited three. There was no discussion or planning beforehand, but he had condoms on him when he showed up. It wasn't like he wasn't thinking about it too.

A wet smacking sound broke my thoughts. I peered over Callum in the direction of the noise, the bunk diagonally opposite ours. On the bottom bunk a large lump bobbed rhythmically under a single blanket. The top bunk was empty. It looked like Diana and Sam were hooking up. I mean, what else was there to do?

Callum looked at me. I could just make out his grin. I wondered if Sally and Wiremu were still asleep. No movement from their bunk. They were on the top of the last bunk set in the six-person room. Wiremu was a mess; he'd sculled his bottle of spirits within an hour of arriving at the holiday park and Sally had to take him to bed. By the time the rest of us came back to the bunkroom they were asleep, or were doing a good job of pretending to be.

Callum and I settled back down. I tried to concentrate on getting to sleep rather than the movement of greasy bodies on a plastic mattress. "Where's the condom?" I asked suddenly. He lifted up the covers to look. A waft of latex and sweat hit my face. His hands found our underwear, knotted and warm. He shrugged. "I don't know." I pulled on my shirt and knickers, and turned to face the wall.

I thought of Sally's birthday party last month. At some point we'd noticed that half the girls she'd invited were missing. Sally opened the lounge door to find them in the hallway, giggling in a tight circle on the floor. We couldn't join in, they said, shooing us away. It was a private discussion. We wouldn't understand; we hadn't had sex yet.

In the morning we woke to find multiple coloured condoms littered around the bunk room.

Sam picked up the purple one. "Sorry, guys, that was me," he declared. I knew it was him, having heard the crinkling of foil and the smell of artificial grape late last night. Diana kept stripping the bunk beds. She either hadn't heard or didn't want to respond. Sally and Wiremu were awake, but still in bed whispering to each other. Sam shrugged and started rolling a cigarette.

Callum picked up our green condom from its hiding place under our bottom bunk. He tucked it discreetly into a chip packet. My cheeks grew hot as I watched him throw it in the bin. I was thankful that the flavour we'd drawn blindly in the night was not a pungent one.

Dumped by the door was Sam's Steinlager box, full of our empties. We counted out one bottle of Smirnoff vodka, four Smirnoff Ice Blacks, four Gordons, three vodka mudshakes and eight Steinlagers. Callum and I took them all to the glass recycling bin. On our way back, we slowed and came to a standstill in the grey courtyard outside our bunkroom. It was our last few hours together, here in Taupō Holiday Park. He was driving back up to Auckland with Sam, and the rest of us were heading back down to Whanganui. School tomorrow.

Callum stood with his hands in his blue jeans, looking out

towards nothing in particular. The tips of his brown hair were like hay, brittle from chlorine. He had always been a swimmer. We'd "dated" once before, in intermediate school, when I still lived in Auckland. I'd call him on the weekends and ask what he'd been up to; his answer was always swimming or gaming.

It wasn't a real relationship back then, unlike now. Back then, if I called in the middle of his game of Counter Strike, he would put me on hold to his favourite Limp Bizkit song while he finished his campaign. He would never remember to pick the phone up again.

Conversation was subdued as our car left the holiday park. I was curious about how far everyone got last night, but waited for someone else to initiate the gossip. We were all waiting. Diana and I sat up front, leaving Sally and Wiremu to hold hands in the back seat. At least that much was obvious. Before this trip they hadn't really hung out, but it looked like they were definitely a thing now.

Diana started things off. "Soooooo. Rose. You and Callum, huh?"

"Yeah, he seemed cool," Wiremu volunteered. It was the first time my friends had met him. I wasn't trying to keep it a secret—we just didn't live in the same city.

"What were you guys up to on the top bunk?"

I blushed. "We . . . had sex?"

Diana screamed, hitting the steering wheel with the heel of her hand.

"What? No way!" came from Sally in the back. I turned to look at her. Wiremu held his hand up for a high five. Excited chatter drowned out the low sweep of passing cars. After everyone calmed down, the questioning switched to Diana.

"Soooooo. Diana. You and Sam, huh?"

"Ugh. Yeah," she said, rolling her eyes. "I gave him a blow job, but I didn't really like him."

Callum called me when he got home. "Sam said Diana gave him the worst blow job of his life last night," he said, laughing.

We shared this laugh together, not knowing what would happen over the next few months. He would break up with me out of the blue. I would push him for details but as he tried to explain he'd sound as confused about it as I was. He would still come down for my school ball, flights already booked. The weekend would be messy. We couldn't help hooking up again and I'd notice that the way he looked at me hadn't changed. Then a new girl would start to leave long posts on his Bebo wall. She'd talk knowledgeably about FPSs and RPGs. I would spend too long staring at her pixelated icon, her pale face and dark eye makeup.

壹

The emperor glides through his court, a swathe of officials in his wake. His silk robes are a deep purple, almost black, with red embellishments on the collar and sleeves.

This silk is gathered from the mouths of silkworms. After their feast of mulberry leaves they dance in a figure-eight pattern, vomiting up gossamer thread.

The purple root of the gromwell plant is harvested for the dye. It's difficult to work with; the dye refuses to take easily. To achieve the same hue as the pale veins of taro, the garment requires at least ten washes.

Hands pull the silk through the water over and over again. The emperor's purple needs more work. It has to reach the intensity of dark violet, the shade of twilight falling on China, united as a nation for the first time.

## 2

Whanganui's main drag is Victoria Avenue, aka the Ave. When I was a teenager, the primary pastime was driving down this street and heckling pedestrians, aka "doing an Ave-y". Carloads would congregate spontaneously at the Gull Petrol Station at the top of the Ave. It was the only place open 24 hours in Whanganui. If it was early enough people would head inside to buy a pie or use the toilet; if not the guys would piss in corners, amber liquid mixing with beer from bottles that were invariably smashed. We would loiter until the night manager's patience broke and he'd chase us off the premises with threats of calling the police.

It was after midnight and Baby and I were sitting under a fluorescent light on the corner of the Ave and Maria Place. I don't remember how we got there, or why we weren't with our friends. I don't remember who kissed whom, but I remember being picked up later and ending up at the house of another boy in my year. At the time I thought it was exciting, kissing two boys in one night. My life finally had the level of excitement I saw in *Skins*.

The boys in my year weren't known by their first names. Baby was the runt of his friend group, shorter and smaller than the rest of them. He was taller than me, but just barely. "Baby" was one of the more benign nicknames people had.

We got together late in our seventh-form year, just before school finished for good. It had been a few months, but the breakup with Callum still felt fresh. I knew from the start that the relationship with Baby wasn't going anywhere. Nor did I want it to. But I had to do something to alleviate my boredom. I wondered if my parents would have reconsidered moving from Auckland if they knew the gallons of RTDs and drunk boys' saliva I swallowed to pass the time.

Dating Baby confirmed exactly what I was trying to avoid about dating in Whanganui. Everyone at school was curious about our relationship, about how far we got, about whether Baby had been immunised for yellow fever. So little happened in our small town that our cross-popularity-level relationship was big news. Girls with Roxy backpacks sneered at me and my SpongeBob SquarePants backpack. I wasn't a social pariah, but being in extension maths meant I was exempt from coolness.

Two weeks after the acknowledgement that we were officially dating, Baby came by my house after a night out. It was more early morning than late night; the black sky was bleaching into shades of navy blue as I opened my bedroom window to let him in. As we made out, my mind played back the expectations and projections of everyone at school. I assumed that he assumed that I'd had sex before. It was common knowledge at school that I'd had an out-of-town boyfriend. Sex had felt like something to get over with so that the speculation at school would end and the gossip would move on to something else.

"Do you have condoms on you?" I asked Baby.

"Yeah, in the car." He paused. "Should I go get them?"

"Yeah, if you want."

He pulled on his blue jeans and black Metallica T-shirt and headed back out the window.

There were unspoken rules about how long it was appropriate to wait before having sex. It depended on so many things: how long you'd been dating, whether you'd had sex before, your relative ages. Back in fourth form, word got out that Lydia had had sex with her older boyfriend, and she didn't come to school for an entire week. I had PE with her friends and in the changing room they talked loudly about how she was a slut.

But by now most people in my year had already had sex,

or at least claimed that they had. One of my friends had only waited a few weeks with her new boyfriend. Her justification was that they had both had sex before, and it's not something you can really go back on. So was this okay? Baby and I had been together for only two weeks, but I'd had sex before. Did it matter that Callum and I only had sex once before he broke up with me?

The window frame creaked. Baby climbed back in, holding a twelve-pack of condoms still in their plastic wrapping. I was fairly certain it was his first time, but I didn't want to embarrass him by bringing that up now. We got naked. I pumped his dick half-heartedly to make sure he was hard enough; his fingers rubbed against me to get me wet enough.

Baby handed me a condom and I pretended to know what I was doing. I pinched the tip, like I'd seen in health class. Thankfully it rolled out the right way. I got on top of him. Like the last time, I didn't really feel anything. Baby made a groaning noise, squeezing his eyes shut. It had been less than a minute. I got off him. He scrunched the condom into a wad of toilet paper. He looked around, holding the wad in his hand.

"Where's the bin?"

"Just put it in your pocket." I didn't want to risk my parents finding it in the bin.

We lay back down in my single bed, sleeping close due to the lack of space rather than the presence of feelings. I thought about having sex with Callum. Funny how the gap between how I felt about them hadn't changed the quality of the sex.

*

The last week of school made everyone sentimental. Signatures were collected in scrapbooks and on our white uniform shirts. In our last ever physics class, Baby walked in and sat as usual in the row behind me. Scrawls covered his shirt. Several of them read "sideways vagina". An attempt to draw a sideways vagina had been made; it looked like a raisin. I had never heard this term before but I knew it had to be about me. Buckbeak also noticed. He started laughing and drawing the class's attention to the drawing. I pointed out that it made no anatomical sense. Everyone was too busy laughing to consider its logical inconsistencies.

The popular girls organised an informal prizegiving, with awards such as "Most Likely to Become Prime Minister" and "Most Likely to Become a Millionaire". They had come up with the nominations for each category and circulated a voting form the week before. During our final lunchtime, all the seventh-formers gathered outside the gym for the ceremony. Awards went to the popular girls and their friends, and the reaction from the crowd walked the line between respect and heckling. I sat with my friends, dreading the award that I knew was ahead.

The nominations were read. "Daniel and Jessica, Diana and Wiremu . . ." I winced as I heard my name. Baby's friends cheered.

Baby and I were announced the recipients of "Cutest Couple" award. I didn't want to get up, but the crowd was insistent. We stood up the front like docile cattle and were presented with blue ribbons. "Kiss!" yelled someone from the crowd. Everyone laughed, and to my horror a chant started up. "Kiss! Kiss! Kiss!"

Baby looked at me. I hadn't seen him wear that expression before. It was an expression for the crowd. These people were his lifelong friends. This town was his home base. High school would be a period of genuinely happy memories for him. For me, Whanganui felt like a toilet stop that had gone on for too long. As soon as I had arrived from Auckland I'd wanted to leave as soon as possible. From here I couldn't tell what the future looked like, but I was sure it wouldn't be like this.

The chanting didn't lose any momentum. I decided it was easier to just give them what they wanted, and leaned in.

At the formal prizegiving, teachers proudly announced that a record number of students were going to university—thirty out of our year of 180. I had never questioned that I would go to university. It was never framed as a choice in my household. Leaving Whanganui for university was about the only thing that my parents and I agreed on.

Once exams were over, I picked up my old job at the Mad Butcher. At eight dollars an hour, it was almost a dollar more than the youth minimum wage. Baby worked for his parents out on their farm; their property was remote enough that they had no cellphone reception. We saw each other when he came into town for the weekend, but otherwise we had no contact. I spent my weekdays texting Callum instead.

Baby and I hardly ever hung out alone. I tagged along with him and his friends, hoping not to draw the last king in Four Kings, a drinking game where the loser had to drink a concoction of everyone's drinks. The other girls acted dumb to win the favour of the boys, who would show off by doing things like opening beer bottles with their eyesockets. I tolerated the company of people like Fire Pants, named for the red hair that supposedly ran over all of his body. He was notorious for cheating on girls, but his friends excused his behaviour with, "He's fine if he's in a relationship." Apparently he never thought he was in a relationship. The lore around his virginity was that he lost it when he was thirteen, to a pair of lesbians in their twenties.

Occasionally people with cool parents would throw big parties out on their farms. These events were ticketed at a few bucks each, with the money going towards sound systems and marquees. At one of these parties, Baby and I walked back up the muddy driveway to have sex in his parked car. We experimented with the front seat and the back seat. Both were equally uncomfortable. In the end, we made do with the back. We were too drunk to drive anywhere else.

Sex hadn't got any better. He never asked if I came, and the way that sex was discussed at school had led me to believe that the female orgasm was something elusive and happenstance, like an unexpected prize hidden in a box you've smashed. I straddled him and bounced up and down, even though it wasn't doing much for me. This night was much like any other, except for the part where a group of guys from our year came across us. The sound of their laughter got closer, and then they started rocking the car. It was too dark to identify them, but they could tell who we were by the numberplate of Baby's white Corolla. After a few minutes of drunk hollering, they tired themselves out. As they left, they shouted at Baby to enjoy himself.

News broke that BZP would be reclassified as a Class C drug at the end of summer. Stardust Creations was besieged by people stocking up. One night on BZP, Baby, Fire Pants, Buckbeak and I drove up Durie Hill to the tower, the highest landmark in town. The tower's 176 internal steps led to a panoramic view of Whanganui. But the entrance was gated shut, so we went up the neighbouring tower elevator building instead.

Fire Pants claimed that the lights of Whanganui formed a crocodile shape. He pointed over to the western suburbs of Tawhero and Castlecliff, their lights tapering to make the tail of the reptile. The city centre was the body, the arc of the Whanganui river tracing the underside of the crocodile's belly. To the far east, Aramoho was the boxy head. We stayed a while on the roof, drinking and talking until the wind picked up and our fingers grew numb. Baby was going home to the farm, so I rode with his friends back into town.

From the driver's seat, Fire Pants asked me how long Baby's dick was. Did he have a baby dick to match his baby stature? Buckbeak laughed. I refused to answer, so they refused to drop me off. The car passed my house.

They asked again, going around the block. I said that it was always dark, I couldn't tell. We passed my house again. They asked for a third time. I announced that I was going to jump out of the car. Laughter came from the front, hiding the sound of me unbuckling my seatbelt. The car approached my house again and I flung the door open. Tyres screeched as the car came to a sudden stop and the door slammed shut from the momentum.

Before they had time to react, I wrenched the door open again and got out. Buckbeak wound down the passenger window. Fire Pants shouted across him, "Hey, don't tell Baby about this, okay?"

I climbed into bed and replayed the events of the evening. There was nothing I could ever say to Baby that would tarnish his image of his friends.

For New Year's Eve, we organised a camping trip out at Ruatiti, a campsite northwest of Raetihi. To get there from Whanganui you have to take the Paraparas, a dangerously windy section of State Highway 4.

By the time I arrived, the campsite was already littered with broken glass. Everyone was six hours into a game of Edward

Scrumpyhands, where a bottle of Scrumpy Apple Cider is taped to each hand, rendering the drinker incapable of doing basic tasks until both bottles are drunk.

Baby acknowledged me by raising a hand, which was bound in clear tape to a round green bottle. I sat next to him and cracked open my first drink. He leaned over and began recounting the evening. The first person to finish Scrumpyhands was Ripper, in just forty minutes. He'd chugged his bottles down because he really needed to take a shit. But he was too wasted to find the toilet and ending up shitting all down his legs, so was he really the winner? Baby laughed, blabbing about Ripper spending a good hour wandering stinking drunk around the campsite with his shit-caked legs before some good cunt decided to walk him down to the river for a wash.

The night passed in a stupor and the next day I woke up roasting in my sleeping bag. A half-hearted attempt to clean up was made and dirty tents were stuffed into car boots. We drove in a slow convoy on the unpaved road out of the campsite. Before we got to the main road, the guys in the car at the head of the pack spotted a burnoff in a paddock. A signal was given, and we parked in a line, twenty metres from the fire.

"What's going on?" I asked.

Baby shrugged. He got out of the car and joined the small group gathered around Judd Nuts. The boys stood with arms folded or hands clasped over genitals, giving encouraging nods to Judd Nuts. He broke the formation and swaggered over to the fire, clutching a silver canister in each hand. About a metre from the fire he stopped and turned around, shooting the crowd a cocky grin. He lobbed the half-empty gas canisters into the fire. The crowd cheered as he ran back.

We waited. No one knew how long it would take. Most

people had left their cars to sit on boots or lean on side doors, but I decided to stay inside. Trills of nervous laughter punctuated the anticipation. After five minutes or so, Judd Nuts decided that maybe nothing would happen, and took a few steps towards the crackling fire.

The sudden sound stopped him in his tracks. It was loud, but not ear-splitting. It had a hollow ring to it, like two metal saucepans colliding. Spatters of laughter started up, led by Judd Nuts. With the entertainment over, we started the drive back for real this time.

Among locals there was a certain prestige to getting through the Paraparas in record-breaking time. There was a story that Fire Pants once drove through them so fast he cheated two police officers out of a ticket. A police officer flashed their lights at him as they caught his red car speeding through Raetihi. Fire Pants pretended not to see and floored it through the Paraparas, getting back to Whanganui *impossibly* fast. So impossibly fast that the police officer stationed at the other end, on the lookout for a red car exiting the Paraparas, had to agree that it was *inconceivable* that someone could drive through the Paraparas that fast. It was a case of mistaken identity—they must be looking for a different red car, one that was still navigating the difficult curves of that stretch of road.

What Fire Pants didn't tell too often was the story about the time he didn't brake enough on one particularly sharp corner, and ploughed through the thin metal railing. The front wheels of his car hung over the edge of the cliff, looking down the valley to the Whanganui River several hundred metres below. Baby told me this tale as we took the same corner. He approached it at a modest 90 kilometres an hour. I gripped the sides of my seat as we passed.

"We're about to go over the Banana Bridge," he said.

"What?"

"The Banana Bridge. It's the only curved bridge in the country."

Baby explained that, because of its concave shape, it could be taken at much greater speeds than other sections of road. His physics seemed flawed, and I didn't understand the significance, but I was not in the driver's seat. The engine of his white Corolla roared as the speedometer dialled up to 120, 150, then 160. We flew out the other side of the bridge. He laughed and I joined in, because what else can you do when you're hurtling at speed through the air? The lift, the elevated glimpse of my surroundings, was a reminder to note the ruddy patch of fallen pines, the bright yellow of flowering gorse. Though the images weren't endearing, they lingered.

The next emperor wears yellow. A deep, rich yellow underlit with tones of red and gold. Not the common yellow, worn by the lowest social class. There is no mistaking the different shades: one for a sweat-stained labourer, another for a gilded ruler.

The emperor perches on a long narrow bench. He looks out into his court, contemplating the Theory of Five Elements. This theory informs his military strategy, the layout of his court. Absently smoothing the surface of his 龙袍 | lóngpáo, he recalls the five elements and their colours:

金 | gold, 白 | a radiant white

木 | wood, 青 | a verdant blue-green

水 | water, 黑 | a lacquered black

火 | fire, 赤 | a bright vermillion

土 | earth, 黄 | an alluvial ochre.

His gaze draws back to the square grid in front of him. The chequerboard of 楸木 | catalpa wood is sandy yellow, speckled by a constellation of pieces in two complementary colours. One half the shade of a bruise, carved from 紫檀心 | red sandalwood. The other colourless and crystalline, a hardened tree sap given the name 瑞龙脑 | "lucky dragon's head".

Some pieces are arranged in a cluster; five or six bursts of red. A safer configuration for the pieces would be a line, like real soldiers. The emperor picks up a new piece. He circles the piece between thumb and forefinger, contemplating the tension between power and control.

## 3

After our break-up, Callum and I continued to text each other on and off. There were times during my relationship with Baby when I talked to my ex more often than I did to Baby. I never told Baby this, and he never asked. I left Whanganui for university and he stayed behind to take a gap year. Neither of us bothered with any official break-up. Unacknowledgement was a natural end to a relationship that felt largely situational.

In the first semester break, Callum flew down to see me. He was taking a gap year too, smoking weed, working at the pool and watching movies. I didn't care to establish if we were "in a relationship". I had moved to Christchurch, even further from Auckland. There was nothing to establish.

"I really wanna make you come," Callum said suddenly, pulling out of me. He looked at me, as if I would know. I shrugged. I didn't know how my body worked either. I had never got the hang of masturbating. He thought for a moment. "It's got to be on 4Chan."

My tiny room was lit up by Callum opening the laptop. He tapped away for a bit then placed it back on the desk, facing us. The video showed a thick-necked man standing in front of a raised platform. On it lay a woman. She was naked from the waist down, while he wore a polo shirt and pressed pants. Her tangerine legs were bent up, giving a full view of her perfect hairless peach. Her face and the top half of her torso were hidden behind the taut swell of her breasts.

The man held up two stubby fingers and explained the two basic hand positions. One was a V for victory. He laid his fingers along the length of her labia, with the apex of the V at her clit. "This is the warm-up position," he said as he massaged up and down. For the main act he closed his two fingers together and rubbed from her clitoris to the opening of her vagina.

Her legs started shaking. He placed his free hand firmly on top of her pelvis, pinning the epicentre of her tremors as he continued to stroke. "She's close," he grinned, looking directly into the camera. She let out a high-pitched whinny. The shoot zoomed to his hand. Back to the first position. "It's better to draw it out for a bit, it makes her orgasm better," he drawled off screen. Fingers slowly worked up and down, up and down. Finally, he increased his tempo. Her back arched as she came, hands trembling by her side. "It's as simple as that!"

Callum shut the laptop. We lay back down on the bed. With his hands he mimicked the man in the video. "Does that feel good?" he asked. I clammed up, being put on the spot like that. I wished my body would cooperate, that it would respond to the same script as the woman in the video. I didn't want to disappoint Callum. It felt good, but how good did it need to feel before I would come? What did coming even feel like? I'd asked a friend once and she replied, "Well, you just *know*."


I flew up to Auckland at the start of the mid-year break. I didn't know at the time, but this would be the last time I saw Callum. I was only there for two days, but we spent most of the first day driving to Hamilton for an ounce. I was in the passenger seat, watching the countryside pass in drabs of green and grey.

Callum parked on a nondescript street to collect the weed. I'd never seen an ounce before. It was larger than I expected, a cloud of green stuffed in a ziplock bag. He exchanged cash for the package and chucked it over his shoulder into the back seat. He reached for the ignition, paused, then reached back to cover the weed with a hoodie.

Our first stop in Auckland was Sam's house. I was relegated to the back seat; they had sales to do. We were on a street somewhere in Blockhouse Bay, the surroundings stark in their ordinariness: weatherboard houses, trees, low wooden fences. Callum used his mum's kitchen scales to weigh out individual grams, him and Sam chuckling about profit margins up front.

Sam's Nokia vibrated as orders came in. Soon a hooded figure sauntered up to the car. He was young, male and white. Shoulders rounding to place his hands in his hoodie's middle pocket. A twenty-dollar note was passed through the window and a foil package given in return. I didn't catch his face, just the side of his pimpled cheek as he leaned in.

After an hour, we finally went back to Callum's house. In his room he rolled a joint and put on a movie. He opened the window and sat on the sill, lighting up and blowing smoke out into the warm Auckland evening. With a hand he motioned for me to sit by him. Smoking weed was another thing I had tried several times but never felt like I got right. I inhaled like he told me to, holding the smoke in my lungs, but I didn't feel any different afterwards. The room was filled with the noise of the movie's opening scene with Jason Statham simultaneously driving and shooting. Callum chuckled, even though we had watched this before.

叁

What unnecessary bloodshed. Zhū Dì shakes his head. His nephew has already been appointed Crown prince. This attempt to consolidate more power by targeting his uncles is pointless. Zhū Dì sighs. His hand has been forced. He is left with no choice but to overthrow his nephew.

Zhū Dì sets up occupation in the imperial palace in Nánjīng. He proclaims himself the Emperor of Eternal Happiness. One arm and then the other is pulled through the sleeves of his new yellow robes. They are embellished with images of dragons, the symbol of imperial rule.

The local scholars are upset. They dispute the new emperor's legitimacy. In a fury, the Emperor of Eternal Happiness purges the scholars, along with nine degrees of their kinship. China's capital is moved to Běijīng.

The construction of a new imperial palace begins. The foreman sources uncut logs of wood from the southwestern jungles, slabs of marble from quarries near Běijīng, golden bricks baked in Sùzhōu. Nine is the number associated with emperors; the emperor boasts that his new palace will have 9999 rooms.

He looks up to the night sky. It's still and cloudless; celestial bodies are dancing, shifting blue and red. But one point remains fixed, that of 紫微星 | the Purple Star. The home of the Celestial Emperor. "As the Terrestrial Emperor, my new palace should be a reflection of the heavenly palace," the emperor muses. He gives his new palace the name 紫禁城 | Purple Forbidden City.

The palace is considered the centre of 中国 | the Middle Kingdom, and thus the centre of the entire world. To symbolise this, the roofs are painted yellow after the fifth compass direction: the middle. Yellow is the colour of the fifth season, the end of summer, and the emperor himself.

From the Táng dynasty onwards, this shade of yellow is reserved for the ruling class. The rest of the social classes follow: purple, dark red, green, blue and down to white.

A girl shows me how to make a daisy chain. She pierces a hole in the stem with her small fingers and slides another daisy through. Holding out her wrist, she asks me to chain the final flower, closing the loop of alternating green, white and yellow.

In the weekend I sit on my lawn, picking and chaining daisies to form a crown. I place it delicately on my head and run inside to show my mum. Her face falls.

"你不能把白色的花放在头上。白色表示死亡，头上戴白花说明你亲人去世了。" | "You can't place white flowers on your head. White represents death. If you wear a white flower, it means that a relative has passed away."

4

James had a penchant for brown jerseys and a habit of turning up late. He was tall and skinny, with a gangly frame that never filled out in the time that we were together. His bones were slightly too long for his body, tendons and ligaments not quite reaching their length. It showed most prominently in his feet, that his connective tissue pulled too tight. Pale toes pinched up to form a mountain range, shiny pink from the rub of socks and shoes. He called them "hammer toes", and would tape them up individually when we went tramping.

We met in a tutorial for a core engineering maths paper. I was the only girl in the class, and had recently decided to date a Nice Guy rather than the clods I was used to. He was shy, so it took a while to get past his reserve. He was funny and kind, and more interested in talking to me than getting wasted with his mates. Over summer break I went back to Whanganui and texted him the entire time. He stayed in Christchurch, at his parents' house where he still lived. He'd spent his childhood playing at the foot of the Port Hills and taking trips to his grandmother's bach in Hanmer.

James came over on my first night back in Christchurch. I led him into my room. There was nowhere to sit other than my bed. He perched on the edge, his arms tucked like a bird ready to take flight. Now that we were back in the same city I wanted to have a physical side to our relationship, not just an emotional one. He liked me, but he hadn't dated anyone before. I was the experienced one, so I made the first move.

As soon as we started kissing it felt wrong, like he was peeling an orange with only his mouth. I laughed and he pulled back, hurt, a flighty look in his eyes. I made a note of his sensitivity, and reminded myself of the times that it had translated to his care and empathy. Rubbing his back, I reassured him and resolved to be more patient.

The physical nature of our relationship progressed, though at a pace too fast for him and too slow for me. I taught him the basics of what to do with his hands. Because of the newness, every touch felt effervescent, though I still hadn't figured out the specifics of orgasm.

I wanted to have sex, and I could tell that he did too. We tried a few times, but there was a point where the expression in his eyes changed, and he slunk out of the moment. I didn't know where he went. I sensed that it had to do with his Christian upbringing. He had only left the church a year ago. When we tried to talk about it, I could see the difficulty in his expression, but he couldn't form the thoughts into words. He told me that before I came along, he was content to be an island. Self-sufficient, isolated, emotionally separate. There were things that wound him up in a tight coil, one he couldn't release.

Sex wasn't the only complication. We were different in so many ways. My brash extroversion to his quiet introversion, his love for video games and my hatred for them. We circled and argued over the same issues again and again. But there was something shared in our humour. Our outlook on the world made us come back together again to reconcile our differences. We learned to ask less from each other.

After a while our arguments were spaced further apart. A pattern formed in which we never talked about hard things. I went to parties and gigs while he stayed at home. We settled on our mutual interests of board games and tramping. Sex between us became more fluid, although I felt ashamed that I had a higher sex drive than he did. He jokingly referred to sex as "servicing" me, and after attempting to go down on me once, he wrinkled his nose and declared he didn't like doing it;

there was too much hair. I got a Brazilian to see if that changed anything, but his hesitation made me too mortified to ask again.

Most of James's family lived in Christchurch. Over time, I was introduced to all of them. First were his parents. Initially I was nervous, having led their only son off the good path and into a life of sin, but they were welcoming. His mum, Chris, had bright eyes and swept-back hair like a lion's mane. She collected cat paraphernalia and teddy bears. The first time I went to their house on Huntsbury Hill, I tripped over a waist-high cat statue on my way to the bathroom. James's dad, Dave, was the type of man who was good with his hands and never wore long pants. He had built the downstairs extension of their house, where James's bedroom was. Despite the lines on Dave's face, his expression was open and childlike.

Their house was always warm. Except in the height of summer, Chris always had the heater going. She was a night owl, whereas Dave was asleep before ten. Whenever James and I visited she would be in the lounge, her pink slippered feet propped up on the two-bar heater, waving us over for a chat. I was curious about her life, as it was so different from mine and my parents'. She told me that she and Dave had met through a home group at church. Their faith had brought them together—the daughter of a university professor and the illiterate son of working-class Cantabrians. One day Chris invited the whole home group over for a roast dinner, but Dave was the only one who showed up. To her surprise, he ate the entire roast beef meant for eight people. Two months later they were engaged, and that was that. She taught him to read and he did up their little house on Huntsbury Hill.

The next family member I met was Bernice, James's grandmother on his mother's side. She lived by herself in a huge house in Cashmere, her husband having passed away a number of years ago. At her house I understood why some kids hated vegetables. She served silverbeet wrung out by a pressure cooker and carrots boiled until they were limp and gummy.

Bernice doted on her children and grandchildren. After the earthquakes her house was among the first to get repaired, though the damage was only cosmetic. Some of the things she said made me suspect that she hadn't associated with non-white people much before. She could be described as "meaning well". She was God-fearing, and her church friends made certain to tell me about their hardworking Asian gardener or the one Asian family that lived down their street.

James's extended family of aunts, uncles and cousins had the same surname as his grandmother Bernice: White. When I met the Whites their eyes widened slightly with surprise, as if they should have been briefed on my ethnicity. When I opened my mouth and spoke with a New Zealand accent, you could feel their relief in the air. Corn on the cob was served for dinner and I ate it the way I always had—meticulously picking off the first row by hand so that subsequent rows could be separated cleanly. I liked leaving a perfectly hulled cob. My family made fun of me for it. Aunty White watched me, then she turned to James and said, "Hey, James, you should show Rose how we eat corn in New Zealand."

James turned to me, gaping like a goldfish. I thought about all the other family dinners to come in the future. If I didn't say something now, chances were it would be harder and nastier in the future. "No one else in my family eats corn this way," I said.

She tittered. "Well. Well, there's no way I would've known that."

肆

My mum started dating my dad when she was nineteen, the same age I was when I met James. 庙镇 | Miàozhèn was a small town. They were three years apart in age but knew each other from school, the only school in town.

In her last year of school, she often came home to the sight of the Lù doctors calling on her parents. They had been visiting a lot. Sometimes they would wave her over and ask her questions: How is your health, how are you going at school, we hear you've been accepted into a university, you must be very bright!

She blushed later when she was set up on a date with their son. She felt naïve to think that their interest had been neighbourly due diligence. He was her first and only boyfriend.

One dinner I asked my parents what they used to do on their dates. My dad grinned playfully, right canine poking out from the corner of his mouth. He put his chopsticks down, lips greasy, and looked at my mum. He leaned in affectionately, trying to hug her from the side.

"通常大家都一样，就是出去一起吃个饭，一起学习之类的。" | "Oh, you know, going out to dinner, studying together, the usual," my mum said, swatting him away with feigned annoyance. He chuckled and tried to hold her again. This time, she let him.

"我也不是他的第一个女朋友。你爸爸会担心他随口说到前女友的约会。" | "You know, I wasn't even his first girlfriend—that's why he isn't answering you. He's afraid he'll accidentally tell you about dates he went on that weren't with me."

She met his impish gaze with a smile. He nodded at me with a mock grave expression. "你妈妈说的都是对的。" | "Your mother is always right," he said, performing several kowtows to her in apology for ever thinking about another woman.

The next day my mum drove me to Palmerston North to catch my flight back to Christchurch. I picked up our conversation from dinner the night before. I couldn't picture my nerdy, jokester dad as the Fire Pants of 庙镇 | Miàozhèn.

"爸爸到底有过多少个女朋友？" | "How many other girl-friends did Dad actually have?"

Mum laughed. "有几个，但是并不是很认真。只谈了几周，最多一个月。" | "Ah, a few, but none of them were very serious. I think they only lasted a few weeks, or maybe a month."

"你认识她们吗？" | "Did you know any of them?"

"认识一个。她是我的高中同学，现在是护士。" | "Yes, one of them. She also went to our high school, she became a nurse."

"他的父母不介意你的爸妈是农民？我还以为家庭背景是中国人在意的事情呢。" | "His parents didn't mind that your family were farmers? I thought status was a big thing for Chinese people?"

"我们都住在农村，大家都很穷。即使他们是医生，他们只是比我们多一些肉票之类的，并没有很大的差距。" | "Oh, we lived in the country. No one had anything of value back then. Even though they were doctors, that only meant that they got a few extra coupons for meat and such, you couldn't notice such small differences."

The conversation paused. I summoned the courage to ask my mother a question I had been pondering for a while.

"结婚之前你和爸爸有没有上过床？" | "Did you and Dad wait until marriage to have sex?"

Her eyes stayed fixed on the road. I watched for any hint of embarrassment in her expression.

"通常来讲合乎常情。我们等到拿到了结婚证。" | "Well, it was always legal. We waited until we had the marriage certificate."

"合乎常情？" | "Legal?" I asked, repeating the Mandarin back to her. I was confused. Did she mean the law permitted it, or that it was socially sanctioned?

She made some more comments but I couldn't follow. The Mandarin she used was too hard, and I was too embarrassed to press the subject further. I leaned back in my seat, wondering if my mother had ever felt like me.

## 5

Chris was a long surviving heart–lung transplant patient. Before the transplant in her early thirties, she was a pale shade of blue from the lack of oxygen circulating in her body.

The new set of organs served her well. In the end it wasn't either of them that gave out; it was her kidneys. Since the transplant she had been on immune-system-suppressing drugs, ones that were hard on the waste-filtering organs. Two and a half years into my relationship with James, he received a phone call from his dad to say that the doctors had given Chris two weeks to live.

James and I were in the last semester of our engineering degrees, and he decided to postpone his final papers to spend more time with his mother. She was started on peritoneal dialysis, and her condition improved. It was still life-threatening, but the prognosis was now more like months than weeks. For months to change to years, Chris would have needed a kidney transplant, but since she had already had a transplant she didn't qualify for the waitlist.

She spent the next year in and out of the hospital, moving constantly between the hospital in town and their house in Huntsbury. Everything else fell to one side. Christmas was Chris's favourite holiday, and she was happy to have made it to another one. I graduated, then I started an engineering job in Christchurch. James delayed university by a further semester, as the papers he wanted to take were only available in the second half of the year. Life settled back into a routine again, just one that incorporated regular trips to the hospital.

Almost a year after the first phone call, her kidneys finally gave out. The family had known it was approaching. In her last week, Dave slept at the hospital in an armchair at her bedside.

On her last evening, James stayed at the hospital until about three o'clock in the morning. I stirred briefly when he climbed into bed, long enough to register a sense of foreboding.

I woke again while it was still dark. It wasn't a natural awakening; my limbs and chest felt like lead. The landline was ringing. Almost no one called on the landline. I looked over at James, curled away from me. He hadn't stirred, he must have been exhausted. I didn't want to wake him. The call must be serious for them to wait for so long. I went to the phone.

"Hello, it's Mary from the hospital. May I speak to James?"

That foreboding came back in a hot flash. "Is it his mum? Can I take a message? He's still sleeping."

"Sorry, dear, you'll have to put him on the phone."

At the time of her death, Chris was two weeks away from the eighteenth anniversary of her heart–lung transplant.

Two weeks after his mother passed away, James called me.

"Hey . . . so, I'm at the hospital . . ."

I cycled the familiar route. He was in the emergency department. He looked up sheepishly when I arrived. Our flatmate Jared had driven him there. James held up his right hand, in a blue cast. He had punched a hole in our living-room wall.

Dave had decided to tell a long-standing family friend that he was in love with her. They had a lot in common, he'd explained to James. She'd also had a spouse who was a transplant patient, and she'd lost him a few years ago. James was furious. He swore at the top of his lungs and punched a hole in our red living-room wall. Grief can make people act in unexpected ways.

Jared was home when it happened. "I've never heard a human make a sound like that," he told me later. With James's broken writing hand, university was put on hold for the third time. Everything began to move on without him. His grandmother knew a manager at an engineering firm with a job for him. He took the number, but didn't call. He stayed in the lounge, curtains drawn. Every day I came home to the sound of gunshots from the Xbox.

After six months I started losing my patience. I was fed up with the lack of anything other than video games in James's life. But I couldn't bring up my dissatisfaction. It felt heartless to demand productivity from him while he was still grieving. I had saved money and wanted to travel, but it wasn't financially possible for him.

I worried about our hypothetical future. It was relatively inconsequential to fall apart now, while we were young and without much responsibility. But what would happen when we were older? This wouldn't be the only hardship if we had a life together. What if we had a mortgage or a kid to support? How would we cope if this was the amount of resilience I could expect from him?

The year after his mother's death showed me the measure of our personalities: what we were like when there was nothing holding us together. Years later, I would look back through my diaries from those five years with James and see the same thought repeated over and over again: "Should relationships be this hard? I'll give things six more months to improve."

伍

The immigration consultancy my parents went through provided temporary accommodation for new arrivals, a block of houses somewhere in Auckland. My family arrived on 1 January in 1996, unaware that the different calendar marked our first day as a public holiday. We had only American bills, having converted our money at a rate of eight to one back in China. New Zealand dollars weren't available in China so it was the next best thing. We knocked on the door next to us. The Tóng family had a daughter my age and lent us cash while we waited for banks to reopen.

Our families moved to Rotorua together, living in the front and back of a partitioned house. Their daughter, Alice, was my first friend in New Zealand. We played together every day in the shared backyard. Against the fence was a grapefruit tree, dropping yellow fruit that deflated soft and brown. A few months later, her family left for Australia; I was too young to remember why. We were six years old, cheeks and limbs like kneaded dough. Alice's parents called her Little Piggy.

In adulthood, Alice and I found each other on Facebook. Her family had settled in Melbourne: more opportunities. I visited in 2012 and she took the train from Box Hill into the CBD to meet me. She told me about the games of make-believe we played, games that I had clean forgotten. We ambled to Flinders Street Station and discussed our future plans.

"I think I'm going to move to Sydney after I finish my PhD. I need to get away from my parents."

"Yeah, I moved out when I was eighteen. I can't imagine what it would've been like to stay with them for so long."

"They're so annoying. They hassle me about my weight, but at dinner tell me I'm not eating enough. And it took me a long time to stop hating my dad."

"Why did you hate your dad?"

She looked at me. "You don't remember?"

I shook my head.

"He used to hit my mum. Your parents definitely knew about it. My mum would go to them sometimes."

"Oh, God. I'm really sorry." How had I forgotten this? I hesitated. "Is it still happening?"

"No. It stopped pretty soon after we moved to Australia."

We reached the top of an overpass that looked out over the train tracks.

"Are they okay now? Did your mum think about leaving him?"

Alice twisted the strap of her shoulder bag with one hand. "We didn't know anyone apart from your family. Where could we have gone?"

I saw her again before I left Melbourne. Her parents asked me to come to a Chinese New Year lunch at a restaurant near their house. I walked in and saw zero white faces. Aunties chattered in Mandarin or Cantonese, while kids ran around screaming in English.

Alice's parents recognised me at once. "哎! 你真的长大了。瘦了很多!" | "Ai! You've grown up! You've gotten skinnier!" her mum said.

I sat down and her parents peppered me with questions about my life. I answered as well as I could in Mandarin. They exchanged happy glances with each other. I didn't know how to feel about this.

I had planned on taking the train and then the bus to the airport, but her dad insisted on driving me. "哎呀, 这里的公交太慢了!" | "Aiya, the public transport here is too slow!"

He paid for everyone and we went to the car. I hadn't expected him to be so affable. For the whole ride he talked about his daughter, life in Melbourne, real-estate prices. I couldn't bring myself to engage with him.

The next time I saw my mum, I relayed my conversation with Alice to her.

"你真的不记得? 哎呀, 有时候他们很吵闹。我们报了几次警。" | "You really don't remember? Aiya, sometimes their fighting would be so noisy. We called the police a few times."

"Did they do anything?"

"他们有什么办法?" | "What could they do?"

## 6

It had been a month since I moved to Wellington. After the dispiriting state of post-quake Christchurch, an ordinary place felt novel. I loved the walkability of the city, the verdant native bush. For the first week after the move I felt guilty about the ease with which I'd forgotten Christchurch and my old life there with James. It felt better to look ahead.

I thought about the past from time to time, checking in with my changing feelings. One night I realised with a jolt that I'd been having sex with the same person for five years. What if I had been doing it wrong the whole time? I reached for my laptop and scrolled through my Facebook friends. Who was someone I knew well enough, but not too well? There. I landed on a boy from my engineering class. Perfect. He wasn't in the same social circle as my other Wellington friends. I waited for an opportunity to present itself.

I was invited to a party just up the road from his flat, in Aro Valley. We planned to go together. The party was small and I didn't know many people other than the host, but it was a suitable place to get drunk. As we left, he suggested I stay at his house if I was too drunk to cycle home. The living room had a couch, but we both knew that wasn't what he meant.

In his room we climbed into bed. We laid facing each other, and closed our eyes under the pretence of sleeping. Our bodies weren't touching but we were close enough that I could feel the static from his forearm hair. He smelled like fresh pine with a lace of alcohol. I became hyper-aware of the measure of our breathing. His hand traced up my forearm and around my waist. I didn't discourage him so he reached under my shirt to caress my naked back.

His movements felt practised as he slowly peeled off my

clothing. His mouth kissed a path down my belly and I was drunk enough not to feel self-conscious about how I tasted, how I smelled. At university he had a reputation for being promiscuous. It was a relief to hook up with someone sexually experienced, who wanted sex for the sake of sex.

Each time we slept together I became more comfortable within my body, and began to understand my responses. I stopped worrying about cleanliness every time his head went south. He treated it like it was no big deal, and I started to believe him when he said he enjoyed it. A semblance of attachment grew between us, but neither of us wanted anything more. He was leaving for Canada in a few months, and I was glad that the expiration date was decided for us. There was more that I wanted to explore.

陆

Olivia opens my textbook and taps the passage we are studying with a pen. She's been my Mandarin teacher for the past year.

"小明，别眼红人家的摩托车，" I read out loud. "眼红?" I repeat. I know that 眼 means "eye" and 红 means "red", but I don't know what they mean together.

"英文应该是 'envious' 吧。" Olivia translates.

"啊!"

In one culture you are green with envy; in another you are red. Olivia asks if I can think of other colours that are symbolically different. I think of white. The traditional Western colour of brides, representing purity and innocence. Despite its origins as a mourning colour, Olivia tells me that many Chinese brides now opt for white weddings over the traditional red.

I think of yellow. In Western culture it can represent cowardice, old age and sickness. But in Chinese culture it means happiness, glory and wisdom; the emperor's colour. The colour of mineral-rich loess, the golden silt that characterises 黄河 | the Yellow River, the birthplace of Ancient China. From the river basin this agrarian culture prospered and grew.

Like that of other colours, the symbolic meaning of 黄 | yellow has changed over time. Its contemporary allusion is of obscenity, indecency. 黄片儿 | "Yellow movie" is the Mandarin term for pornography. I imagine it's named for the colour of the people on the screen, naked and writhing in their full yellow glory. Maybe this is why we are coveted, sought after for our radiant appeal. They want to lie in our reflected light.

## 7

After James and I broke up, Mum sent me an email. I was surprised. She had never done anything like that before. We weren't a family who talked so directly—we didn't even call one another very often. Her email was written entirely in Mandarin, and she provided English translations in brackets for vocabulary that she thought I wouldn't know.

The email expressed regret at our break-up, but said that ultimately it was for the best. Five years is a long time, my mum mused, but we think that he wasn't good enough for you. She then outlined five criteria that my future suitors must meet. I laughed out loud; they were ridiculous. "He must have a university education and earn more than you, lest he feel inferior." And: "He must come from a nice family with good work ethic and no hereditary diseases."

I appreciated the sentiment, but I didn't know what to say. Our views on life and relationships felt oceans apart. A week later my mum called to ask if I had received the email, as I had never replied.

In the years that followed, the email would pop into my head now and again. Sometimes after a bad date, sometimes out of the blue. For my parents, sexual and romantic attraction weren't the only factors to measure a relationship by. I had never seen my parents kiss, but I thought of how much their marriage had endured. A new country, a new language, years of instability with work. Their relationship had a utilitarian element. It was a way of sharing the load, of holding steady.

The freedom I had to choose my romantic relationships was gained through my parents' efforts for upward mobility. Did they cross the Pacific Ocean just so I could learn how to have a good fuck? But they'd made the best choice they could given their circumstances, and I was making the best choices I could given mine. I just had more choices.

I search my inbox for the email. It's been five years since I last read it, and it is more tender than I remembered. The first criterion for a suitable boyfriend was: "He must love you wholeheartedly, protect you and look after you."

Being looked after was never something I had desired. But I understood that my parents didn't mean for me to give up my autonomy and be kept indoors. They simply wanted someone to care for me as much as they did. Someone to cook for me, someone who could share the burden during the hard times. Someone who could accompany me where my parents couldn't.

柒

Empress Dowager Cíxǐ watches as her five-year-old son is appointed to the position of emperor. Her elevation to empress dowager is also new; upon the old emperor's death, he promoted her and Empress Cí'ān to the rank of empress dowager, and instated eight regents to support the new emperor until he came of age.

She scans the court for the oval face of Empress Dowager Cí'ān. Her long-standing friend meets her eye. Throughout the old emperor's battle with dementia, these two women have controlled court affairs. She sneers as she turns to watch the eight fools dressed in blue. Do these regents think they could obtain power easily?

While the empresses dowager wait for an astrologically favourable time to return to Běijīng, they gather their allies and plot a coup. To remove the regents from power, Empress Dowager Cíxǐ rewrites history. She accuses the regents of gross incompetencies, and alters the records to reflect her claims. The eight are overthrown. In order to display her mercy, Empress Dowager Cíxǐ kills only three of them. One regent is beheaded, while the other two are delivered bolts of white silk. The cloth pulls silky and tight against the regents' necks, coming as a respite from their prison cells.

Empress Dowager Cíxǐ stands behind the curtain with Empress Dowager Cí'ān. The emperor officiates the passing of his first royal edicts. One of them states that the empresses dowager are to be the sole decision-makers, without interference. The child emperor fidgets in his heavy ornamental gear as he looks back at the curtain. Empress Dowager Cí'ān smiles at him.

For the next two decades, the women split their duties

in accordance with their preferences. Cíxǐ, the shrewd and analytical thinker, handles the state affairs. Even as her son reaches governing age, he acquiesces to his mother's superior political strategy. Among her achievements is the abolition of slavery, the Five Punishments and foot-binding. Cí'ān is left to her literary pursuits and is lauded for her excellence with the honorific "Literary Empress".

The two women occupy palaces on opposite sides of the Forbidden City, but come together to sit in the many gardens. Holding cups of tea, they look out into the water lapping the pagoda's edge. They see piles of craggy rock, willow branches twirling in the breeze, their reflection as sisters.

## 8

I met Jade at a party in Aro Valley. She was my height, with short brown hair, and she made sustained eye contact. After she left the party I recognised a familiar hitch in my chest, and thought about her clear green eyes.

A few weeks later we had lunch at Fisherman's Plate and talked about our plans for the Christmas break. Coincidentally, we would both be in Thailand. I was going with my dad and brother, while she was travelling with her ex-girlfriend. We planned to meet up in Chiang Mai. The hour's lunchbreak was up, and our spoons scraped the bottom of our bowls of phở.

The next time I saw her was at her birthday party in Newtown on a rainy Sunday afternoon. One of her friends motioned to me as I arrived. Jade greeted me with a huge smile and I slunk in to stand by her side. She whirlwinded around the room, giving me so many new names I immediately forgot them all. She had as much energy as the seven-year-old she introduced me to.

After the festivities quietened, Jade asked if I wanted to keep hanging out. We went back to my house and discussed dinner options. Jade wanted to make pasta from scratch. She was so enthused about it that I forgot that I don't like pasta. My flatmate watched with a bemused expression then closed the door to the kitchen to give us space. After dinner we retreated upstairs to watch *Bob's Burgers*.

She sat close enough to me in bed that I could smell her, could see how soft her skin was. Her eyelashes were long, faint freckles on her cheeks. I tried not to let her catch me looking, but I noticed that she was looking too. It couldn't be that different really, could it?

We kissed, and her head and her mouth were so small I

felt like a giant. In actuality we were about the same size, but I wasn't used to her finer features, her downy hair. I felt self-conscious about the sweat slicking my palms, the dampness building on my skin. She mumbled something about not wanting to give me the wrong idea by having sex on the first date. I laughed, telling her that it was fine.

She taught me what to do with my hands, and as I tried to mirror her I felt clumsy. Her knowledge of her body was exacting, she knew exactly where to direct my attention, which motions were working, when to stop. I felt inexperienced and she reassured me it would get easier. She got on top and pressed her thigh against me, leaning her hip into my groin. I ran my hand through her short hair as her tongue thumbed over my clit.

After we finished I noticed that I still felt a throbbing in the crease of my leg. Jade must have pressed too hard. I told Jade and she screamed, half in apology and half in laughter, hoping that this sex injury hadn't put me off sex with women.

The next day we both called in sick to work. Avoiding the possibility of being seen in town, we decided to go to the zoo. We walked hand in hand, and it felt awkward for some reason. I realised I'd been accustomed to having my hand at the back; my hand was always held rather than doing the holding. We passed groups of mothers pushing strollers uphill. They stared at us, much more than I was accustomed to.

With Jade, I caught myself exhibiting small strange behaviours. The first time we went on a road trip, I automatically handed the keys to her. She looked at me with the keys in her hand, asking, "Do you want me to drive?" On days we didn't see each other she would call me. James had never liked phone calls, so the first few times she called I answered in a panic, assuming that something was wrong. I went down on her and thought, I'm not sure what my ex's problem was.

Christmas approached and we formulated a plan. Things were getting serious, but I was reluctant to tell my family unless we were heading into marriage territory. We came to a compromise when she met my dad and brother in Chiang Mai.

To my dad I said: "This is my friend Jade. I'm going to stay with her instead. But we'll meet up with you and Matthew during the day."

To my brother, Matthew, I said: "This is my girlfriend, Jade. Don't tell Dad."

We had it all figured out. I would introduce her to my parents as my friend, and they could get to know her. She would learn Mandarin and charm them. It would be easier for them to accept she was my girlfriend this way.

In my teens, I had proposed a scenario to my mum. "如果我是同性恋你会接受吗？" | "Would you accept me if I was gay?" I asked her.

"可是你不是同性恋。" | "But you're not gay."

"那如果我是呢？" | "But if I were?"

"你不是。" | "You're not gay."

捌

Empress Dowager Cíxǐ becomes forlorn after the sudden death of Empress Dowager Cí'ān. Governing alone, her court addresses her as 老佛爷 | Old Master Buddha, the title reserved for Qīng dynasty emperors. She huffs through the court restless and companionless, eunuchs scattering like flies on her approach.

Cíxǐ decides to open the palace doors and invite women to sit with her in the Forbidden City. The invitation is passed far and wide, and among the guests is an American portrait painter, Katherine Carl. For the first time in history, Cíxǐ welcomes foreigners.

In her private chambers Cíxǐ dresses for her portrait. A new robe has been commissioned for this purpose, canola yellow with a black trim. Cí'ān would have approved. Over her gown Cíxǐ drapes her favourite item of jewellery, a lattice cape of pearls. Hair next. She passes over the Manchu headdresses arranged on her dresser, and opts instead for a large winged headdress of her own invention. In her old age she needs a headdress that requires less hair to stay in position. An ornamental hairpin, tasselled with jewels, pins the black velvet base of the headdress in place.

The sitting room for the portrait is furnished with wood as dark as obsidian. Against this backdrop, Cíxǐ's yellow robe gleams. She settles in a carved seat in front of the artist, and her attendants even out the patterned front of her dress.

Katherine Carl wears a plain set of robes for painting. She looks at the woman in front of her. Cíxǐ is composed and level, her power palpable in her unwavering gaze. They call her the Dragon Lady. Around her is a wreath of phoenixes, suspended in flight.

## 9

The route from Shànghǎi to 庙镇 | Miàozhèn spans multiple forms of transport: a subway ride to the wharf, a boat across the Yangtze river, and a bus to 庙镇 | Miàozhèn. In total the journey is almost four hours. At every stage the amount of 崇明话 | Chóngmíng dialect I hear increases. It's only my third time back to 崇明 | Chóngmíng since I left, and the first with a companion: Tom. We met two years ago at one of Jade's parties. By then, Jade and I had been broken up for about six months. I'd never broached the topic of our relationship, and my sexuality, with my parents.

The bus stops a block away from my grandparents' apartment. Tom and I walk the long way via the fruit shop. My mum has briefed me on the basics of filial piety: Take them some fruit and sit with them; they're old so just do what they want to do. We pick out a large watermelon and some pearly grapes.

My uncle is waiting for us outside the apartment. I haven't seen him since I was eight. He looks exactly as I remember, the same broad face and spiky hair as my dad. He clasps Tom's hand in greeting.

My grandparents' house is sparsely decorated. A dining table occupies the majority of the space in the small lounge. On the table are ten different dishes, including egg dumplings, stir-fried local vegetables, the classic red-braised pork, and sweet-and-sour spare ribs. In the kitchen sits a wicker tray of wontons to make the staple food. My grandma and grandpa are sitting waiting at the table.

"Shiao-ngi!" | "小怡!" they call out to me. My grandma rises unsteadily to hug me. I receive a wave of love, familial and unearned. When I pull back, her eyes are pooling. I was the grandchild who spent the most time in her care, and she looks at me fondly.

"这是 Tàng," I say, giving an approximation of Tom's name. "奶奶好," Tom says politely. They look at him, nodding and smiling. My grandpa gestures for us to sit and eat. In lieu of verbal communication, I've told Tom that the best way to show appreciation is to eat as much as he could.

"你爷爷四点起床，去早市买菜。" | "Your grandpa got up at four o'clock in the morning to go to the market for groceries," my uncle says. I relay this to Tom and he nods to my grandpa in thanks. Another piece of vegetarian chicken is placed in his bowl.

My grandma gives a wheezing cough. She pokes out her tongue, fanning it with her hand. "Ghe za su-ji 'la lai le!" | "This vegetarian chicken is so spicy!" she exclaims. My dad had told my uncle that Tom liked spicy food, so he added chili to dishes that were normally served plain. Tom glances at me, mortified, but my grandma laughs, mollifying the spice with more rice.

The pace of eating slows; there is too much to get through. We have made a sizeable dent, but my grandparents have deliberately over-catered. They wanted to cook everything I would have missed from my hometown. My uncle starts clearing plates from the table in preparation for dessert, and my grandpa goes to his room.

Tom tries to get up to help but my uncle shoos him away. We sit and wait at the table, smiling at my grandma. A red envelope thuds in front of us. My grandpa sits back down, motioning with his eyebrows for us to take the envelope. Tom looks to me. I reach for the packet, adorned with a giant 囍 | double happiness, in golden foil. It's thick. I hesitate. I don't know if it's impolite to open it, or impolite not to open it.

I open it. I peek inside and see a neat stack of bills. By their reddish colour I recognise them as hundred-yuan notes. I close the top flap. The decorative front faces me, and with a start I notice some other phrases: 永结同心~~花好月圆.

"Oh, no," I say. I try not to let the panic show on my face.

"What?" Tom says.

"They think we're getting married."

"What?!" he whispers.

"The packet. It's a wedding packet."

Tom turns it over. "Should we refuse it?"

"I think that would be more rude."

"What do we do, then?"

I pause and glance up to see if my grandparents are watching us. "I don't know. Let me text my mum."

I keep my eyes on my grandparents as I rummage in my bag under the table. My hand closes around the rectangular object. They look at me impassively. Shit. I've only spoken English since the envelope arrived. I let my phone go, and bring my empty hands back up to the table.

"谢谢爷爷奶奶," I say, and Tom follows suit. In return my grandma pats our hands, while my grandpa gives a modest shake of the head. My grandma looks cheerful, but there's no detectable change in my grandpa's expression.

The red packet sits between us and my grandparents while I send a WeChat message to my mum. From the kitchen I hear the rupturing sound of my uncle halving a watermelon.

"你们喜欢吃西瓜吗?" | "Do you like eating watermelon?" I ask.

My grandpa grunts in affirmation. My grandma nods, and turns her head expectantly to Tom.

"我喜欢吃西瓜。" | "I like eating watermelon," he says to her.

My phone lights up. I whisper the reply to Tom. "My mum

says that we should take it. They're getting old, it's better to let them believe that we're getting married. It'll make them happy."

Tom shifts in his seat. "Well, it's your family, so your call."

I take the envelope and slip it into my bag. I was sick of the loud red catching my eye. A plate of watermelon lands with a thunk on the table. "吃吧!" | "Eat!" my uncle proclaims, and the attention turns back to food.

After a walk around the neighbourhood, we head back to Shànghǎi. It's been only a short visit to Chóngmíng, but there isn't space for us to stay out here. My cousin is sitting in the kitchen when we arrive back at her house. She laughs at us as I tell her the events of the day. "当然! 当你见对方的爷爷奶奶的时候意味着你们要结婚了。" | "Of course! When you meet the grandparents it symbolises that you intend to get married."

"诶? 我妈妈为什么没告诉我?" | "Eh?! Why didn't my mum tell me that?"

"我也不知道。可能她认为这种传统习俗对你不适用, 因为你在国外长大的。" | "I don't know. Maybe she thought that the traditions wouldn't apply to you anymore, since you've been away from China for so long."

I pose the question to my mum. She sends me back a voice message.

"我忘了。" | "I forgot," she laughs. "呆在国外太久了, 我没想起来这个习俗。" | "These old customs aren't present in our minds anymore."

Under the patrilineal succession system, women technically could not rule. However, many empresses dowager controlled the state before their child emperor came of age. The practice was given the phrase 垂帘听政 | "ruling from behind the curtain", referring to the charade in which the empress dowager would stand behind the emperor, hidden by a screen, directing his rulings.

The designation 皇帝 | emperor is the title given to the supreme autocratic ruler. Their words were thought to come direct from the heavens. Only through translation does this term gain a gender; a constraint of languages that lack a gender-agnostic word.

Over two millennia of dynastic history, only one woman has been formally recognised as 皇帝 | emperor. This 皇帝 | empress lived in the seventh century. Her birth name is unknown, but she assumed the name Wǔ Zétiān after her coronation. Highly educated from a young age, she was ambitious and knowledgeable of government affairs. Like many powerful women in history, she had been criticised harshly by scholars. Despite her irrefutable prowess with state affairs, she had been scrutinised for her seizing of imperial power.

Her son, Emperor Ruìzōng of Táng, was on the throne when it was yielded to her. She was granted the title of 皇帝 | empress and declared the beginning of a new dynasty: the Zhōu dynasty. She believed herself to be a direct descendant of the ancient Zhōu dynasty, the longest dynasty in Chinese history. Even before this display of officiation, she had the authority and the appearance of 皇帝 | empress.

While Emperor Ruìzōng still reigned, she sat beside him in proceedings, whispering proclamations into his ear. He would parrot her words to the officials, functioning as her mouthpiece. She refused to hide behind a curtain. Wǔ Zétiān sat in full view of the court, resplendent in the emperor's yellow.

# THE TIGER CUB

You were born on a Sunday. I woke up in the bedroom I shared with Mum and Dad, and found that they were gone. This wasn't unusual; I was accustomed to being left alone occasionally while they negotiated work and study.

I got myself out of bed and went to the fridge. For breakfast I chose the carton of sugared doughnut holes from the Pak'nSave bakery. The living room was dim but my parents said to keep the curtains closed if I was home by myself. I settled in front of the TV. *What Now* was on. That's how I remember that the day you were born was a Sunday.

When you came home you needed to sleep in the room with Mum and Dad, so I moved into the study. Both my wishes, for a sibling and my own room, had come true at once. All the other kids at school had siblings; how nice it would be to have someone to play Chinese chequers with.

But the reality of having a baby around was that my parents had even less time for me. I contained my resentment for the first few weeks, but one morning before school I snapped.

Since the baby, Mum and Dad had been too busy to make me a hot breakfast even once. I burst into tears, wailing that they didn't love me anymore.

The load eased when our grandparents arrived in New Zealand, and this little hiccup was forgotten. As soon as the month of confinement for mother and child ended, I pleaded to take you into school for Show and Tell. I was so proud to have a new little brother.

Nine years and four months is the gap between us. You were born in 1999, the Year of the Rabbit. Dad is also a rabbit. Mum and I are horses. In personality, though, I take after Dad: animated, gregarious, in constant motion. And you're more like Mum: quiet, acquiescent, a content homebody. In pictures of Mum in her youth, when she had short hair, she looks exactly as you do now.

Our differences started out young. You were easy to raise. Obedient, staying exactly where you were left. Whereas at kindergarten in China, I scratched up a kid so badly they were taken to the hospital.

The only real discipline you received was a trick that Mum used to play when you were a toddler reluctant to go to bed. She would tell you that a family of tigers shared our house. They were a family like ours, with a mum, a dad and two cubs. As evening fell, they left the forests where they hunted during the day and headed to our lounge to make their beds for the night. In the morning, Mum would get up early and chase them back outside. Such was our agreement with the tiger family. I was a natural co-conspirator. Sometimes you would hear this story, pout, and ask, "为什么姐姐不去睡觉?" | "Why does older sister not have to sleep?"

"姐姐大了, 老虎怕她了。" | "Older sister is big now, the tigers

198

are afraid of her."

I exchanged a glance with Mum. "这一家老虎很凶呀! 牙齿
很尖!" | "The tiger family is very fierce! They have such pointy
teeth!" I would say to you, eyes wide and arms raised for effect.

Your mouth set with fear. You would let Mum pick you up
and carry you out of the lounge, leaving me in the company
of tigers.

My semi-parental relationship with you continued when I
moved to Christchurch for university. I convinced Mum
and Dad to send you down to visit me in the overlap of our
holidays. For a week I cooked dinner for us and drove you
around the city.

One of my flatmates had gone away for the break and let
you have his bed. In the mornings I went to wake you up and
was taken aback by the length of your body. When did you
get so tall? In my mind you were still my little brother, with a
small body I could lift and carry. But at ten years old you were
about to surpass me in height.

As soon as you became tall, you started to make yourself
smaller. "Matthew 站直!" Mum would bark, pressing your
shoulders back with her paws. For a moment you would raise
your head and bring your neck back in line with your spine. It
was a small improvement to your posture, but your shoulders
were still up by your ears, maintaining the hollow at the centre
of your chest.

I felt a sharp obligation to protect you from—or at least
warn you about—the perils of growing up in Whanganui with
our parents. Mum and Dad were inclined to say things like,
"最好你们俩的性格换一下。你真不像女孩, 一整天在外面疯玩
儿, Matthew 也不像男孩, 赶也赶不出去。" | "It would be best
if you two swapped personalities. You're not at all like a girl,

199

spending your days outside like a wild child. Matthew's not at all like a boy—we can't ever get him to leave the house."

When Mum said that, I rolled my eyes and looked at you. Your face bore a wooden expression. From about fourteen you wore this face, with downcast eyes and hard lips and cheeks. I couldn't tell if you were internalising their statements or simply ignoring them. You had never been talkative, but as a teenager you became taciturn in that stereotypical way.

We went on long walks around the neighbourhood so we could talk freely. The conversation always felt hard. I didn't want it to be so one-sided, me spouting opinions to counterbalance what you were hearing from Mum and Dad, but no matter how much silence I left, you would never fill it. Affirmatives were the most I ever got from you, when what I wanted was some reflection to show that you had understood.

Perhaps I was looking for too much. I couldn't put myself back in the mindset of my teens to assess whether I would have been capable of such a conversation. I could never tell how the conversation was going for you. Your face was impassive, drained of any emotion. Did it feel patronising, in the way that any received wisdom does at that age? But you must have enjoyed our conversations enough to keep agreeing to go on walks. All I hoped to do was reassure you that it was safe to speak to me, and trust that you would reach out if you needed to.

If my friends asked about you, I would often say, "Picture someone who is the complete opposite of me." It wasn't just our personalities—our experiences were completely different. My childhood was one of upheaval. I attended five primary schools, one intermediate school and two high schools. Your schooling was all in Whanganui.

After intermediate, you were sent to a private school and started going to compulsory chapel every week. Every evening and weekend, you were busy with school activities. If it wasn't some sort of sports practice, it was an extension maths or science class. The focus at my public school was simply to pass; your school demanded excellence.

Either implicitly or explicitly, I imagine that your school told its students that they were important and would achieve great things. Your peers had iPhones and went overseas in the holidays to spend time with their parents who worked in multinational companies. They strolled through the manicured grounds with innate self-assurance and high expectations for all aspects of their lives.

In Year Eleven you started rowing. Your arms and legs swelled like bean pods, skin pulled tight and shiny. You gained about fifteen kilos of muscle. It hung on you like a heavy cloak you were yet to feel comfortable in. The way you held yourself hadn't changed. You still hunched, shoulders collapsed over your sternum, making yourself seem small even though you no longer were.

Mum and Dad never had time to hang about at your rowing practice, so they sent me along one Saturday morning. Gazebos were set up at the riverside. Under the constructed shade, white dads flipped patties and white mums brought out containers of baking. I was the only sibling there, and I didn't know which category of white parent would be more interesting to talk to.

Boat after boat skimmed past on the Whanganui River. They came in ones and twos, young men pulling in unison. Sitting on the bank, I was too far away to be able to distinguish you from the rest of the pack. How natural did it feel, I wondered, to perform these long strokes? Dressed in the same black and blue, looking like one of the team.

I talked to a few of the rowing mums and idly sampled cupcakes. They tasted homogenous despite the colour range in their pleated cups. Our conversation died fairly quickly as I didn't know their families or sons, and the types of questions they asked weren't ones I wanted to elaborate on. I folded the waxed wrappers into quarters and then eighths as I looked at the dads behind the grill. It would be nice to have something productive to do with my hands.

At the end of practice the boats were hauled out of the river and stacked in the boat shed. You were silent amid the throng of young men coming up the bank. Their banter was a combination of boasting and teasing, the same coarse yells I remembered from high school. One-upping each other in the number of muscle-ups they could do. Girls' names thrown around like paper into a wastebasket. The word "gay" used as a pejorative. Ten years had passed since I was last in school, but the Lynx Africa masculinity was yet to be retired.

As soon as the tidying was done you grabbed your stuff, ready to leave. A chorus of byes came from your teammates, as well as a sharp laugh that I couldn't interpret.

"You don't want to stay and eat some sausages with your friends?" I asked.

You gave me a look. We both knew that lunch would be much better at home.

We wandered towards the parked car. "So, are you friends with those guys?" I asked.

"Not really."

"I guess they're quite different, huh?"

"Yeah."

*

Did you know Dad believes that auspicious events occur every seven years? Well, give or take. Once he marked out the beats of his life to the cadence of seven: going to university in Shànghǎi, leaving China for New Zealand, buying the shop in Whanganui. There are a few missed beats in there; places where he was too young or too tied down to seize the opportunity waiting for him.

According to his rough calculations, 2018 was the next big year. I think he was right. It was a big year for the entire family. Our parents prepared to sell the shop. I went back to university to do my master's. You moved out of home and started your first year of university.

In my head I picture you walking the path I abandoned. You enrolled in a bachelor of health sciences at Otago University, and had a room at Carrington Hall. It was the same degree and hall of residence that I was accepted into ten years ago. Before you left home, you packed your things in the same purple and black suitcase I had used.

The Lù family had always been doctors, except for Dad and his brother, who didn't do well enough in the 高考 | gāokǎo to go on to study medicine. Our dad was the smarter of the two, and from practice tests it looked likely that he would succeed. But on the day he got sick and underperformed, so that was that. At the time, it wasn't possible to retake the 高考. Everyone was granted just one opportunity to improve their future through education. Like his older brother, he had to settle for being an engineer instead.

Of their children, I was the first to secede from studying medicine. I didn't even start the undergrad degree. Simon, our only cousin, got much further. He completed a biochemical engineering degree in Canada as his pre-med requirement.

Next came the medical college admission test and interviews. He failed to get in. So he retook the MCAT and the interviews at the next opportunity.

In total, he failed to pass the day-long medical entry exam seven times. At this point, he was forced to stop because he had reached the lifetime restriction on number of attempts. If it were up to him, maybe he would still be taking that exam now.

Dad joked that you were the last member of the family left who could become a doctor. I didn't know how seriously you took his words. I suspected that, like me at your age, you had no idea what the other options were. Back then, the only adults I interacted with were teachers, our parents, and my coworkers at the Mad Butcher; none of their jobs seemed like a good fit for me. I was a smart kid so traditional professions like medicine, law or engineering seemed like the way to go. They were jobs I understood only in the abstract, but no one around me could offer a useful description of what they were really like. It wasn't until after I moved to Wellington that I understood the array of options I had at that time, but also the avenues that were never open to me.

For years you expressed ambivalence towards the idea of enrolling in med school. But in Year Thirteen, you became fixed on the idea. I assumed the pressure came from Mum and Dad, but they said it wasn't their influence. They had reassessed your suitability for medicine, and, given your introverted nature, concluded that your bedside manner would be inadequate. But you were firm in your choice, even though you couldn't explain it to me when I asked.

"I dunno. I think it's interesting," you replied in your usual muted way. Two sentences were about all that you verbalised of your decision. Were you drawn in by the prestige of med school? Was it pressure from other kids who aspired to go there?

Did you feel a need to prove yourself? Your motive was a mystery to everyone. Regardless, I was excited to see you leave home. Life was going to change and improve in ways you couldn't have understood at the time.

I wanted us to speak more often, but we weren't in the habit of messaging, so it was hard to start up out of the blue. From a distance it looked like you were having a good time. I liked a picture of you going to the toga party with a group of friends who were all of Asian heritage.

Mum kept me updated on how you were. Her news revolved around assignment grades and exam results. Many of our parents' friends had children enrolled in first-year health sciences. It felt like Mum and Dad were keeping closer tabs on your grades than you were.

My first year at university featured midweek absinthe shots and missing nine o'clock lectures. But during your first year you were chained to your desk. Your first lecture was at eight in the morning and you'd study until eleven every night. Eleven was considered an early bedtime. Other students claimed to be up until two or three, studying hard and psyching out the competition with their unfaltering work ethic.

If you weren't studying you were reading posts on the med school forum, a place for students to post their grades and share their experiences. At the end of the year, the moderators of the forum would reverse-engineer the exact grade average needed to gain entrance to med school. Acceptance had such a narrow rate of success, and every year thousands of capable young people were crushed by these impossible standards.

We would go months without talking, but I was never worried. I had assumed that a lack of communication meant that you were fine. Late one evening on the cusp of spring, you sent me a four-page document through Messenger. I had never known you to write. On the page you spoke with no ums or ahs, no hesitation, no maybes. Your voice was suddenly clear and eloquent.

"I've never really been able to say everything I've wanted to when I talk to someone about my mental health," you wrote. "I always end up chickening out just before I say it. I can chalk that up to how awkward I am. The amount of time I've wasted just dwelling on what I'm going to say is ridiculous, especially considering I don't even end up saying half of what I intend to . . .

"Trying to piece together exactly how I've been feeling over these past months is difficult. What I'm trying to get at is that I'm not sad. At least that's not the whole story. Depression is a lot of different feelings. None of them are good. It's an exhaustion that keeps me in my bed all day. There's no drive, no motivation to go out and live my life. It's a haze that blocks out everything good in the world and leaves me alone with my self hating thoughts. Let's steal an analogy. 'Physically it feels like I have the flu. Mentally it feels like I deserve the flu.' . . .

"I was depressed in high school. Probably. Might have been teen angst that I'm overblowing but whatever. I think a lot of the reason I've found it so difficult to talk about is how unaccepting we are of mental illness. The label of depression carries so much weight. That's in the past now though. I've got friends that are willing to support me through this. It's not like everything is fixed now though. I'm still so terrified of talking about this. This way of thinking has been burnt into my head. It's why I waited so long to tell you. Part of me is still plagued with so much doubt and paranoia that I freeze up every time I talk about my mental health . . .

"Recovery has been tough. I think it's because of how much

of it is on me. I described it to my therapist as being as if we treated broken legs by having the patient run a marathon. She found it pretty funny. I'm trying my best and that's all I can really ask for at this point. I guess I viewed therapy as this cure-all that would magically take all my problems away. All change pretty much has to come from me."

My initial reaction was a feeling that I had failed you. Were there signs I should have seen earlier? Being quiet wasn't necessarily an indication of troubles, and neither was a lack of strong camaraderie at high school. We weren't people who suited Whanganui, but I had forgotten how bleak that felt at the time.

I assessed the severity of the situation through the counselling basics I had learned at Youthline. Were you at risk to yourself? No. Had you sought professional help? Yes, you had gone to the doctor and been prescribed antidepressants and referred to a counsellor. Did you have good support networks? It sounded like you had good friends, despite your self-effacing words about being awkward. I resolved to call you every week.

"Do you think you understand your feelings?"

"Yeah."

"Okay, what things make you happy, or sad?"

A long pause.

"I dunno."

"Well, do you think that conflicts with what you just said? About understanding your feelings?"

"Maybe."

Our phone calls were like pulling teeth. I hoped you were chattier to your counsellor. I broached the idea of you telling Mum and Dad how you were feeling. Mental health wasn't something that they had a good grasp on, but I thought it would be different if it was their own kid. They would need to get better at talking about it.

Understandably, you were hesitant about the idea.

"Maybe," you replied.

I thought about the last time I tried to raise the topic of mental health with Mum. She had been recounting a newspaper article to me, about a successful and beloved doctor in Whanganui who had died by suicide. He was active in his community, cheerful and kind.

"我不理解。" | "I really can't understand," Mum said, shaking her head.

I got that heat in my chest, the one that accompanies the expression of something important but difficult. In English I could have said something articulate, but all I managed to spit out was "这些东西表面看不出的。" | "You can't spot these things."

She looked at me, giving a half chuckle. "你不是说你有过 depression 吗?" | "You're not saying you had depression, are you?"

"不是。" | "No." But I wanted to say that I had been close to people who did. I saw how it sat on them, how they had to keep dragging it around. How you might need to learn how to manage it for the rest of your life, rather than ever putting it behind you for good.

"Matthew 这学期一直在生病。" | "Matthew's been sick this entire semester," Mum announced as soon as I got into the car. We were heading to the airport to pick you up. Your first year at university was three quarters of the way through.

"他说晚上一直睡不着觉, 每天上课很累。医生给他配了点儿 药, 可是没有什么用。唉, 我看他这个状态可能考不上医学院。" | "He can't get to sleep. He's tired in class every day. The doctor prescribed him some medicine, but it hasn't had any effect. Ai, in this condition I don't think he'll be able to get into medical school."

What an interesting half-truth you had told her. She spoke in a rush, fitting as many details as she could in the fifteen-minute drive to the airport. She seemed more concerned about the impact of the illness on your studies than about how we might help you to recuperate. Reading between the lines it was obvious what shape your illness had, but Mum appeared to have taken your words at face value. Like me, you had a hard time lying.

This was to be the first time I would see you in person since you'd written to me. I prepared myself for a lack of apparent change in you, but I was still unsettled by how routine your behaviour was. We went to yum cha and you ate heartily, having missed breakfast due to sleeping in.

"Matthew 你看上去长胖了。现在体重多少?" | "Matthew, you look like you've gotten fatter. How much do you weigh now?" Mum asked, pushing the plate of 扣肉 | steamed pork closer to you.

"I dunno," you replied.

"是不是太用功学习了, 没时间去跑步?" | "Is it because you're studying too hard, you don't have time to go running?"

You gave a half-nod, half-shrug. I changed the topic. You had a full week ahead of questions like these. After lunch you and Mum were heading back to Whanganui while I remained in Wellington. It wouldn't be until Christmas that all of us were together.

In those intervening months, you spent the days sleeping in and not leaving the house. Socialising had never been a priority of yours, but these holidays you were more withdrawn than usual. Part of it was exhaustion; you needed to recover from the stress of the year.

I worried about your situation. Your school friends were back for the holidays, but you didn't even send them a message. One of the friends you were planning to flat with the following year lived in Wellington, so I offered you the fold-out couch at my place, but you never organised a bus ticket to come down. The most I could wheedle out of you was an agreement to come tramping with me and my friends over the New Year. From a young age you had preferred the company of people older than you.

Exam results were released a few weeks before Christmas, with letters of admission to follow. It wasn't looking good. Your grade average from papers alone sat in the nineties but it wasn't enough to make up for your middling score in the UMAT, a three-part test on logic, empathy and non-verbal reasoning that was notorious for being difficult to prepare for.

Each year, the cut-off became higher and higher. There was speculation that there were even fewer places available this year, because the programme was accidentally oversubscribed last year. It was not a lucky year for your cohort of students.

Three days before Christmas, it was confirmed: you had not gained a place in medicine, and you hadn't even made the waitlist. I could measure Mum's worry by the number of WeChat voice messages she left me. She described you moping around the house, your face a downturned mask. Everyone in the house stepped carefully around you, afraid of doing anything to upset you any further.

Given your results, Mum thought the best course of action was to start over with a new degree—perhaps engineering at Canterbury. You weren't interested, though. You wanted to finish your bachelor of health sciences and reapply for medicine. You wanted a second chance.

*

At Christmas, everything seemed normal at home except for the boxes dotted around the place. Our parents and grandparents were preparing for the big move. From 2019, the Year of the Pig, they would live in Auckland. You glanced up from your phone and said "Hey" as I came into the lounge carrying Tom's and my luggage.

Dinner that night was a little off. Dad was his usual self, yanking open the top cupboard to get the 白酒 | báijiǔ, but Mum responded by rolling her eyes. Thankfully no one broached the subject of your future.

The next morning, Mum cornered me in the kitchen. The shop was quiet and you hadn't woken up yet. "你知道爸爸昨天跟 Matthew 说什么吗?" | "Do you know what your dad said to Matthew yesterday?" she said. "男子汉要持之以恒。" | "Men need to persevere."

I didn't know Dad still held out hope for a doctor in the family.

Mum continued, "今年你看他的身体弄成这样。这么大的压力他受不了了。让他再这样子两年, 他肯定坚持不下来。" | "Look how bad his health has gotten this year. He can't cope with this much pressure. Two more years like this, he definitely won't cope."

You found it patronising when your counsellor partly attributed your depression to university, but there was some truth to it. In the second half of the university year you went to the dining hall for dinner, alone, just before it closed. That way you didn't have to waste precious studying time chit-chatting with your friends, and you could have a double serving of dinner as there were no further students to feed.

Mum was furious when she heard about this behaviour. Better exam results weren't worth this self-enforced isolation.

She was trying to make me her accomplice again, but this time you weren't a toddler.

"你们徒步的时候一定要跟 Matthew 好好的聊一聊, 他不能继续读这个专业了。" | "When you're tramping you must have a proper chat to Matthew. He can't keep studying this degree."

She didn't have confidence in your ability to make your own decisions and to come to terms with failure. I agreed to talk to you, but not to convince you of anything. Shrugging, I reminded her how ineffective her attempts to discipline *me* were. Unlike when I was a teenager, I could see that her concerns came from a place of care, but instead of working with you to understand what you were going through, she had skipped forward to what she thought was a solution.

At the root of her worry was your health. It felt like we were circling around the topic of depression, getting closer to establishing a common vocabulary to talk about it but not quite landing in the same place. In the past, her understanding of the concept of mental health had been simplistic. She could sympathise when somebody had an emotional response to significant trauma, but she couldn't understand a condition that was an underlying, simmering discomfort, or something that came and went, needing constant attention and management. This time it felt different.

"你知道医生给 Matthew 开了什么药吗?" | "Do you know what type of medicine Matthew was given by the doctor?" I ventured.

"不知道具体是哪一种, 但是他说是可以帮助睡眠的。" | "Not the specifics, but he said they helped him sleep."

"他不让我告诉你, 可是药是 antidepressants." | "He told me not to tell you, but they were antidepressants."

She paused, lips parting and closing again. "我问了赵叔叔。" | "I asked Steven about this," she said, speaking of our family friends, the Zhàos, who were doctors in China. "我担心弟弟变胖了, 就想知道哪些药会引起发胖。我跟赵叔叔描述了弟弟的状况, 他说听起来像是 antidepressants." | "I was worried because Matthew was getting fat. What sort of pills can make you fat? I described his symptoms. Steven said that it sounded like antidepressants."

Then she said, "我们一辈子已经吃了这么多苦, 就想要你跟弟弟的日子过得舒服一点。你劝他转个专业, 没必要走这条路。" | "We have eaten so much bitterness in our lives just so that you and your brother could have more comfortable days. You have to persuade him to change his degree, he can't keep walking down this path."

*

Our tramping route circled Mt Ruapehu, passing through beech forest, lahar zones, desert terrain and brisk springs. All going to plan it would take six days to walk the track. The four of us—me, you, Tom and Kezia—drove in two cars.

In the first half of the drive you rode with Kezia. If it had been a different friend I would have worried about the potential for it to be awkward, but Kezia had a knack for making people feel comfortable. In Tūrangi we stopped to carb-load on pies and chips, and swapped passengers. The next leg was you and me, cocooned in the front seats.

Our lives had diverged at such a young age, and from what I could glean about your first year of university we had continued in these opposing directions. The moments that held significance for you, the ones that built into a series of quiet acknowledgements about the world, were yours alone to untangle. I waited to hear what you had made of it so far.

"I'm going to finish health sci, and think about whether I want to re-apply for med."

"Yeah, you've said before that some people prefer completing the bachelor's so they have more time to think about doing med?"

"Yeah. And second and third year aren't as hard as Mum and Dad think. I've talked to a bunch of second and third years and they all said first year was the hardest."

"That makes sense. What do you think you'd do if you don't get into med again?"

"There's a postgrad degree in biomedical engineering at Auckland Uni that looks interesting, I'd probably do that."

I chuckled to myself. It looked possible that our family was moving away from medicine permanently.

"There's the master's in creative writing I did last year as well, in Wellington. I think that's something you could do."

"Hmm. Yeah, maybe."

The conversation stilled for a bit. We turned a corner and Mt Tongariro came into view.

"Hey, did you end up going to the doctor in Whanganui? Surely you would have run out of antidepressants?"

"I stopped taking them before I left Dunedin. They weren't really doing anything, so my doctor told me to stop because of the side effects."

"Oh, okay. How are you feeling?"

"Fine."

"Do you feel better than you did in the middle of the year?"

"Yeah."

"You seem happier."

"Mmm."


On the tramp, you were happy to take your share of the group food but you wouldn't think to do the cooking or cleaning up. At first the rest of us took care of it—there wasn't a lot to do, and it was quicker to just do it. On the third day, I told Tom and Kezia that we shouldn't shy away from giving you specific cooking and cleaning jobs. I washed the plates from dinner and gave them to you to dry. The motion of your two hands around the rim of the plate had a staccato pattern that gave away your inexperience.

"When you make the chore roster in your flat, make it a job for someone to go around and remind everyone else to do their chore for the week," I said.

You nodded.

By the fifth day you automatically got up to help when someone started to collect the dishes. You were chatty when you got talking about something, usually to do with human biology, and you slid in the occasional zinger. Even though your year had been hard, I noticed that you smiled more. You would squeeze your eyelids at something particularly funny, and your eyes looked like tadpoles, tails shaking with delight. Your posture was better too; perhaps this was because you stopped rowing.

It felt like I was watching you flicker between two versions of yourself. As you continued to build confidence, your quiet nature became more contemplative, more self-assured. I couldn't divine what was ahead of you, but I knew your future self would be capable of handling it.

After the tramp, we stopped in Hawke's Bay to visit Sylvia, my yoga teacher, to lengthen our hamstrings back out again. She watched as you walked into the studio, and directed you to the mirror. You were wearing your black rowing shirt and shorts; the only exercise gear you own. Sylvia stood behind you. She took a strap and placed it around your upper arms, rolling them back and down so that your sternum, collarbone and chin would lift.

Your arms were pinned backwards and your shoulders drawn down. Sylvia pulled the strap tighter, winching your arms back even more as you looked directly ahead.

I looked at your reflection. Your shoulders were broad, much broader than I thought they were. Your expression was neutral, unafraid of the space that your frame occupied. And in your chest centre was your heart, open and ready.

# A Note on Languages

I grew up in a bilingual household. My grandparents spoke 崇明话 | Chóngmíng dialect, and my parents spoke 普通话 | standard Mandarin. While I refer to 崇明话 as a dialect in this book, in reality there are no concrete conceptual differences between languages and dialects. The classification is often a semantic issue. In Chinese history, the designation of 普通话 as a language and everything else as a dialect was a political decision.

One of the major changes within the Cultural Revolution was the creation of 普通话. This new language took its pronunciation from the Běijīng dialects, vocabulary from 官话 | the speech of officials and grammar from 白话文 | written vernacular Chinese. Before this, there was no mutually intelligible spoken language in China. For more background on the history of 普通话, I suggest reading *A Billion Voices* by David Moser.

Since 普通话 was adopted as the official language of China in 1909, there has been a substantial loss of linguistic diversity in China. Languages have had different rates of attrition. Cantonese, for example, has remained popular due to geography and Cantonese-language media. But other languages have not been so lucky. As is the case in my family, it is common for younger Chinese generations to have only rudimentary skills in their ancestral languages. In recent years, there have been movements to preserve these languages before the knowledge dies with the native speakers. Romanising my grandparents' 崇明话 in this book is mine.

崇明话 belongs to the 吴 | Wú family of languages, spoken in the area encompassing the municipal of Shànghǎi, most of Zhèjiāng, southern Jiāngsū and small regions in Ānhuī and Jiāngxī. As 崇明话 was spoken on 崇明岛 | Chóngmíng island, it developed without much influence from neighbouring dialects. 崇明话 has retained the eight tones from the Táng Sòng dynasty, compared to Shànghǎinese, which has kept only five.

The romanisation system that I used in this book is one created by 吴语协会 | the Wú Language Society. I am not an expert in 崇明话, and the romanisations I provided are my best approximations from the phonetic system 吴语协会 | the Wú Language Society devised. In China, 崇明话 is localised to one island; in Aotearoa it is even more isolated.

All 崇明话 in this book is displayed in normal text. This was a deliberate choice to break the grammatical convention in which 'foreign' words are italicised. For those of us who have grown up with several languages, this signifier is meaningless. In this book I wanted to centre a multilingual perspective, a world view that is more common than English grammatical conventions would lead us to believe.

# Works Cited

p. 51: "In a blog post about going back to the Four Square in New Plymouth': Serena Chen, "Your Local Dairy Girl", *Serena* (blog), 10 February 2019. serena.nz/writing/local_dairy_girl/

p. 82: "Graci Kim, an Auckland-raised writer, talks about her experience completing a writing assignment": Thalia Kehoe Rowden, "Emerging YA Fiction Writer Graci Goldhart", *The Sapling*, 27 April 2018. thesapling.co.nz/single-post/2018/04/27/Emerging-YA-Fiction-Writer-Graci-Goldhart

p. 88: "Emma Ng's book *Old Asian, New Asian*": K. Emma Ng, *Old Asian, New Asian* (Wellington: Bridget Williams Books, 2017).

p. 89: "As the writer and musician Kristen Ng has observed": Kristen Ng, "Started from the Bottom Now We're Here: 14 Years Since the Poll Tax Apology", *Kiwese* (blog), 11 February 2016. kiwese.co.nz/2016/02/11/poll-tax-apology-reflections/

p. 90: "I found Helene Wong's memoir *Being Chinese*": Helene Wong, *Being Chinese: A New Zealander's Story* (Wellington: Bridget Williams Books, 2016).

p. 94: "At the IIML, all three wrote what would become their first collections of poetry": Nina Mingya Powles, *Luminescent* (Wellington:

Seraph Press, 2017); Chris Tse, *How to Be Dead in a Year of Snakes* (Auckland: Auckland University Press, 2014), Gregory Kan, *This Paper Boat* (Auckland: Auckland University Press, 2016).

p. 95: "the millstone of *but is this authentic / representative / good for black / Asian / Latino / native people?* hanging from their necks": Jenny Zhang, "They Pretend to Be Us While Pretending We Don't Exist", *Buzzfeed*, 12 September 2015. buzzfeed.com/jennybagel/they-pretend-to-be-us-while-pretending-we-dont-exist

p. 96: "In her lecture 'Poutokomanawa'": Tina Makereti, "Pouto-komanawa: The Heartpost" (The University of Auckland Free Public Lecture, Auckland, 17 May 2017). anzliterature.com/feature/poutokomanawa-the-heartpost/

p. 98: "I wonder what life in Aotearoa will be like in 2038, when our population is projected to be a third Māori, Asian and Pasifika": Stats NZ, "Ethnic Diversity Projected to Rise", 18 May 2017. stats.govt.nz/news/ethnic-diversity-projected-to-rise

p. 185: "Empress Dowager Cíxǐ": For a fuller discussion of this empress and how she came to power, see Josep Maria Casals, "Cixi, the Controversial Concubine Who Became Queen, Led China into the Modern Age", *National Geographic*, November/December 2016. nationalgeographic.com/archaeology-and-history/magazine/2016/11-12/profiles-china-empress-dowager-cixi-emperor-guangxu/
To view portraits of Cíxǐ and her hairpiece, see Fang Zong, "The Chinese Manchu Headdress", *Stories from the Museum Floor* (blog), 15 June 2018. storiesfromthemuseumfloor.wordpress.com/2018/06/15/the-chinese-manchu-headdress/

# Acknowledgements

I can't imagine writing this book without the support of these amazing people. My deepest thanks to the following people:

My family for the chain of events that eventually led to this book. 爸爸妈妈，没有你们的牺牲就没有我今天所得到的成就。是你们一直以来的支持让我拥有了更好的未来。谢谢你们用你们的方式让我感受到你们的爱。你们的付出诠释了中国的那句古话："父母之爱子，则为之计深远。" 爷爷奶奶，谢谢你们对我从小到大的呵护。

陆杨帆 | Matthew, you've got your own book somewhere in you.

Ashleigh Young, Fergus Barrowman, Kirsten McDougall and the rest of the team at Victoria University Press for the production of this book. Thank you for taking so much care with the formatting and type for all three of the languages, and granting me so much trust to bend and invent grammatical conventions.

林頌恩 | Sharon Lam for cackling with me about idiosyncratic aspects of Wellington, New Zealand and the diaspora. Thank you for the incredible job on the cover. Thank you for taking everything the right amount of seriously.

My MA class of 2018: Alie Benge, Anna Rankin, Catherine Russ, Charlotte Forrester, Glenda Lewis, Madison Hamill, Susanne Jungersen and Tim Grgec. I can't wait to see all your works out in the world. Thank you for making it a year full of laughter. Extra shout out to Charlotte Forrester for reading a proof of this work and Anna Rankin for being such an important friend and support.

Chris Price for supervising this work, and your meticulous edits.

Thank you for creating a space to explore ideas, and the breadth of knowledge that you brought to workshop.

陈丹婷 | Serena Chen for epitomising my target audience—1.5 generation Chinese migrants who have grown up in the regions—and your constant cheerleading of my work. Thank you for your response to these essays in their draft forms and reminding me who my audience is.

卞安若 | An-Ruo Bian for shaping a lot of my early thoughts about modern China. I admire the pride and love you have for China and New Zealand, and the willingness and patience you show towards others on their cultural journeys.

李晶, my current Mandarin teacher, for your help with the translations, and providing cultural context that I could not have gained through research. Thank you to all the other Mandarin teachers I have had in my life.

*The Pantograph Punch* for publishing an earlier form of the title essay. Thank you for creating a platform that generates such sharp writing. Special thanks to Hannah Newport-Watson for suggesting the title "All Who Live on Islands"; it's a blimmin good one!

The editors of *Sport* 46 for publishing "穷人店、富人店"; it was overwhelming to be published in such fantastic company.

The editors of *Turbine Kapohau* 2018 for publishing an extract from "Cleaver", and Nikita Tu-Bryant, Adam Macaulay and the team at RNZ for turning it into such a great radio piece.

Louise Wallace and Francis Cooke at *Starling* for all they do for young New Zealand writers and for asking me to be a guest author. Thank you for publishing an excerpt from "Yellow Fever".

陈家豪 | Kah Chan for being a great sounding-board for questions of layout and typography.

Eamonn Marra and Freya Daly Sadgrove for their help with a particular essay.

The writers around me who have been generous with their support and guidance. Thank you to all the Asian New Zealand writers who have come before me.

All of my friends who have cameos in the book, and to all the friends who I love dearly but didn't fit into this particular narrative. You're all bloody wonderful.

Tom Wilson for your unwavering support of me at every stage. Thank you for reading countless drafts, and giving such insightful and valuable feedback. This book wouldn't be the same without your clear judgement and willingness to explore ideas with me. I love you. And thank you for doing the most important job of all: making sure I'm never hungry! Thank you for cooking such a great 辣子鸡!